D0354215

JOHN
MUIR

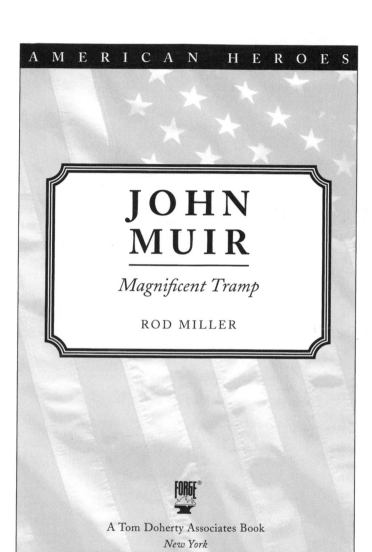

AMERICAN HEROES

JOHN MUIR

Magnificent Tramp

ROD MILLER

FORGE®

A Tom Doherty Associates Book
New York

JOHN MUIR: MAGNIFICENT TRAMP

Copyright © 2005 by Rod Miller

Foreword copyright © 2005 by Dale L. Walker

The author is grateful to the John Muir Papers, Holt-Atherton
Special Collections, University of the Pacific Libraries,
copyright © 1984 Muir-Hanna Trust, for permission to reprint
the frontispiece photograph of John Muir.

Book design by Michael Collica

A Forge Book
Published by Tom Doherty Associates, LLC
175 Fifth Avenue
New York, NY 10010

www.tor.com

Forge® is a registered trademark of
Tom Doherty Associates, LLC.

Library of Congress Cataloging-in-Publication Data

Miller, Rod, 1952-
    John Muir : magnificent tramp / Rod Miller.— 1st
hardcover ed.
        p. cm. 3227 5082 7/05
    "A Tom Doherty Associates book"
    Includes bibliographical references (p. 195) and index
(p. 199).
    ISBN 0-765-31071-6
    EAN 978-0765-31071-2
    1. Muir, John 1838–1914. 2. Naturalists—United
States—Biography. 3. Conservationists—United States—
Biography. I. Title.
QH31.M9M55 2005
333.72'092—dc22
                                            2004030228

First Edition: June 2005

PRINTED IN THE UNITED STATES OF AMERICA

0 9 8 7 6 5 4 3 2 1

Dedicated to my mother,
Renee Miller,
who seldom told me
to get my nose out of a book

Contents

Contents

Foreword

When a young man, John Muir crafted intricate clocks and other clever devices from wood, and once even invented machinery to mass-produce rake and broom handles. But, a Muir legend claims, this gifted woodworker so loved trees that he could not himself cut into a living one.

While there must have been occasions when he had to chop down a tree, each time he did so he probably first gritted his teeth and apologized to God. A great mission of his life, after all, was to see to it that there were more live trees than dead ones to serve mankind, and to this end he influenced four United States presidents to think of living trees. Benjamin Harrison preserved 13 million acres; in 1897, Grover Cleveland set aside 21 million acres of sheltered forest lands; William McKinley contributed several million more; and Theodore Roosevelt signed bills to protect 148 million acres of forested wilderness.

(Muir even loved trees that had turned to stone and in

1906, owing largely to his influence, his friend President Roosevelt designated Arizona's Petrified Forest a national monument.)

"Everything in nature seemed to fascinate him, boy and man," Rod Miller says of this valiant conservationist, and indeed, from his boyhood days on the wild and foggy North Sea coast of Scotland to his death in 1914, Muir saw a spirit-rejuvenating quality in the "inventions of God." By this he meant *all* the inventions: Trees were a passion but he loved all plants, all animals, birds, fish, and insects, rivers, mountains, canyons, deserts, glaciers—every creature and feature of Mother Earth—and he stood in awe and wrote poetically of rain, snow, wind, lightning, earthquake, avalanche, and all the grand, terrifying, and inexplicable forces of nature.

Nothing thrilled him more than witnessing, as he often did in his Alaskan journeys, a glacier violently birthing icebergs, or finding a rare flower, or standing alone and silently on a Sierra peak gazing at a valley below. He thus learned the redemptive value of the wilderness but not from armchair musings or deep readings in philosophy. He was invigorated by the natural world by traveling it, mostly on foot, a knapsack on his back, sleeping under the stars.

The romantic images of him—as the sinewy man of the mountains with the flowing Old Testament beard, or the magnificent tramp walking a thousand miles from Kentucky to the Gulf Coast of Florida, or brewing tea in the High Sierras while studying a plant specimen with a magnifying glass—are faithful concepts. But in this eloquent book, Rod Miller has ensured that we see all the other John Muirs, all of them fascinating.

There is the Muir who once said, "No truant schoolboy is more free and disengaged from all the grave plans and purposes of ordinary orthodox life than is me," but who, because of the grave plans and purposes of others, was forced into the uncomfortable role of combatant. As he rose from obscurity to become a voice for the preservation of the wilderness, he had campaigns to wage, people to convince, and had to engage in national debates, often acrimonious, with politicians and industrialists. One of his finest, final, battles—which he lost—was for the preservation of the Hetch Hetchy Valley, second only to Muir's beloved Yosemite in pristine beauty, against efforts to submerge it under a reservoir to supply water for San Francisco.

There is Muir the scientist, whose explorations of the Yosemite Valley, his uncanny ability to read the runes of canyon walls, convinced him that the valley was formed by glacial action and not by sudden cataclysmic upheaval, the theory accepted by the scientific establishment. For this idea, one opposing scientist called him an "ignorant shepherd," but the shepherd was anything but ignorant and his idea prevailed.

There is Muir the reluctant author who found writing painful and a poor vehicle for describing real experience, but who wrote profoundly and poetically in ten books and in the nation's most influential magazines and newspapers.

There is Muir the private, reclusive man who avoided crowds, speechmaking, and the public spotlight, yet who organized the powerful Sierra Club in 1892 and served as its founding president, and who became the "father" of the National Park System. (Only Yellowstone preceded his efforts.)

And there is Muir the lucky husband, married to an extraordinary woman who gave him two loving daughters and who encouraged his roamings, enabling him to declare his cosmic citizenship, his freedom to wander, and to identify himself as "John Muir, Earth-planet, Universe."

Ralph Waldo Emerson kept a list of men who had influenced his life, a list that included the name John Muir. The two met only once, when Emerson visited Yosemite in 1871 with Muir as his guide, but corresponded until the New Englander died in 1882.

What did this sheltered philosopher and poetic genius see in the untamed, idealistic man of the mountains that was so influential? Emerson did not elaborate, but a safe answer is that he admired Muir's daring, courage, nobility of character, and his selflessness—all the essentials of heroism.

DALE L. WALKER

JOHN
MUIR

A Place in History

I f American history were a bookshelf, the story of John Muir's productive life would tuck conveniently between the volumes on the Civil War and World War I.

He left home for his first trip of any significance as an independent adult in the fall of 1860 to exhibit his handcrafted wooden clocks and other inventions at the Wisconsin State Agricultural Society Fair in Madison. Within months of his departure, the Republican candidate for president, Abraham Lincoln, won election and Southern secessionists pulled the trigger on the Civil War.

Largely silent on the subject of the war years, Muir spent them as a student at the University of Wisconsin or tramping about and working in Canada. One of his younger brothers fled to Canada to dodge the military drafts sweeping Wisconsin, since the family lacked the means to buy a deferment or pay for a substitute—the customary means of draft avoidance at the time. Muir later followed him across the border, where

he spent his time hiking and camping, identifying and studying plants in the forests near the Great Lakes. He later joined
his brother and the pair worked together in a Canadian
sawmill and wood products factory as they awaited the war's
conclusion.

By today's standards, Muir's avoidance of military service
might be judged a cowardly or unpatriotic act; at the time,
however, it was neither unusual nor even necessarily frowned
upon. The draft was unpopular and draft riots were widespread, and circumventing conscription, by legal means or otherwise, was commonplace. Moreover, service may not have
been required of Muir as he was not a citizen of the United
States—he did not apply for formal citizenship until many
years later when, at age sixty-five, he needed a passport to
travel outside the country. In any event, his name was never
drawn for conscription.

Of Southern Reconstruction, Muir had little to say despite
traveling widely throughout the South in 1867 and keeping a
notebook that included passages on the people he met. He
wrote only occasionally, and then briefly, on the political and
social climate, his comments on those topics primarily short
accounts of widespread rural poverty, homelessness, and the
wandering ne'er-do-wells who infested the country. He wrote
that he was once mistaken for one such by a local sheriff who
"could not determine by my colors and rigging to what country
or craft I belonged." The lawman gave Muir to understand
that "since the war, every other stranger in these lonely parts
is supposed to be a criminal, and all are objects of curiosity or
apprehensive concern." Fortunately, the sheriff finally determined him to be harmless, and even invited him into his

home. The notes from the Southern journey later became a book, *A Thousand-Mile Walk to the Gulf,* posthumously published in 1916.

His adult years in America encompassed the completion of the transcontinental railroad, the cattle drives out of Texas that established the country's enduring cowboy myth, and the opening of much of the country's interior to settlement and homesteading. He lived during the Indian wars of the Great Plains and the Southwest, the Spanish-American War, the arrival on American shores of more than twenty-five million immigrants, the loud and lively movements for women's suffrage and temperance that marched (often hand in hand) across the land, and the disenfranchisement of the black populace and the undoing of much of Reconstruction. In brief, he lived through many of the decisive, pivotal events in the unfolding of modern American society and history—not one of which seems to have attracted his interest or attention.

One event, however, did. As the Industrial Revolution mechanized America in the years following the Civil War, change and upheaval cascaded across culture, politics, industry, and agriculture; a sweeping transformation that would not slow down for decades to come. Factory technology improved productivity and created the need for legions of workers, drawing population off the farms and into the cities; developments in agricultural technology allowed farmers to produce greater yields with less labor, resulting in increasing production of food and fiber even with the loss of labor to the insatiable manufacturers. Growing urbanization and clockwork factory schedules created an unprecedented demand for leisure activities. More economical methods of mining and lumbering allowed more efficient exploitation of natural resources, many of which were located in the wide-open spaces of the West, a region becoming less wide-open with the arrival of tens of thousands of settlers.

The consequences of these radical changes rippled across America with the force of tidal waves, sweeping aside a way of life and creating another, newer version in the backwash.

Capitalists reigned supreme from the postwar years until near the turn of the century. Few in government were inclined to meddle in matters of business and economy, so, given free rein, "robber barons" rode roughshod over America's workers, farmers, consumers, citizens, and resources. Illegal syndicates and combines stifled competition, creating monopolies that manipulated supply and demand at the whim of the manufacturers. Prices for raw materials were fixed, wages and hours nonnegotiable, working conditions harsh and unsafe, profits for finished goods predetermined and achieved at all costs.

This world, upon which John Muir chose to turn his back and walk away into the wild, was not easily left behind. The effects of it soon enough reached him in the guise of wasteful and destructive logging of forests, overgrazing of open rangeland, large-scale mining operations that created widespread desolation, and land-grabbing magnates turning vast tracts of public land into personal playgrounds or private storehouses of timber, grass, and minerals—the raw materials that fueled a capitalist machine run amok.

Such excesses eventually became a bitter taste in America's mouth, however, and through a series of reforms near the turn of the twentieth century the people began spitting out the status quo. Populists championed the rights of ordinary people, and progressives, promoting change for the benefit of all rather than the privileged few, gained political influence and then, for a time, control. It was a difficult battle, pitting the zeal and emotion of common folks against a well-financed, firmly entrenched establishment determined to protect its power. The struggle saw workers demand a say, through labor unions, in how they worked, under what conditions, and what they were paid; farmers fought to reduce the stranglehold the railroads and the manufacturers had on freight rates and markets; the public demanded preservation of their forests and scenic treasures.

This struggle to protect and conserve land and resources consumed most of John Muir's adult life—he attempted to right the wrongs he witnessed with an exuberance based on an uncommon affection for Mother Earth. This adoration was given voice throughout his writings, in which he humanized plants, animals, even rocks with thoughts, feelings, emotions, and even a mystical spirituality. In his love for nature and his efforts to protect it, Muir was very much a man of his time— indeed, a man ahead of his time.

The Man in the Boy

Born on April 12, 1838, in Dunbar, Scotland, John Muir grew up there on the shores of the North Sea, some thirty miles east of Edinburgh, until emigrating to America with his family at age eleven. His was an adventuresome childhood, chronicled in his 1913 book, *The Story of My Boyhood and Youth*. In spite of—or perhaps because of—harsh schoolmasters and an even harsher father, the boy never missed an opportunity to cut loose and run free. For these daring exploits, which Muir and his childhood pals called "scootchers," he absorbed punishment at home and at school.

Yet it is in the boy's dare and double-dare scootchers—racing across the hills, scrambling along the seashore, scaling walls, climbing peaks, creeping through hedges, exploring hidden corners—that we see the reflection of the man to come.

Many years in the future, Muir would walk a thousand

miles through the woods and mountains and swamps of the South to the Gulf Coast of Florida just to have a look around. Later, he would hike and climb the length, width, and height of the Sierra Nevada mountain range of California. He would tramp through the arid Great Basin, over countless mountains and valleys. He would undertake seven expeditions to Alaska, the first in 1879 and the last in 1899, to explore the glaciers and mountains, tundra and seashores. His mountaineering skills were formidable—clambering up canyons, scaling cliffs, finding his way with finger- and toe-holds across sheer rock faces, leaping and scrambling across boulder fields—his ingenuity and strength taking him places where few men—and, in some places, no man—had gone before.

How much of this skill was learned on the tumbledown walls of Dunbar Castle, the thousand-year-old ruin that dominated the history of his hometown and the imaginations of the local boys?

"We tried to see who could climb highest on the crumbling peaks and crags, and took chances that no cautious mountaineer would try," he said. "That I did not fall and finish my rock-scrambling in those adventurous boyhood days seems now a reasonable wonder."

What may be Muir's most famous Sierra exploit also has its youthful counterpart. In December 1874 a severe storm caught him in the Sierra Nevada range near the Yuba River and rather than rush for shelter, he "lost no time in pushing out into the woods to enjoy it." He admired the wind whipping the tree branches, and the music of the air rushing through them, and determined "that it would be a fine thing" to climb one of them. He sought out the highest tree on the tallest ridge, squirreled through the branches of a Douglas spruce (a variety of evergreen since renamed Douglas fir) to a perch a hundred feet above the ground, and rode out the storm for several hours "like a bobolink on a reed." As his windblown perch traced an arc across the sky, he tuned into the equally wild variation in the music, exalting in the sounds of the wind strumming the needles of spruce, fir, and pine trees; leafless branches of oak; thickets of laurel and manzanita; even, he claimed, blades of grass.

One night, in Muir's boyhood Dunbar days, we see the shadow of his tree ride. "In search of good scootchers," he opened a dormer window and climbed out onto the roof of the house as the wind bloused and ballooned his nightgown. Thinking it great fun, he lured his younger brother David out to join him. Not wanting to miss a good scootcher, the younger brother was soon astraddle a dormer, then the two scaled the steep slate shingles to perch atop the roof's highest peak in the howling wind. John made it back down the pitch and into the window but David, lacking something of his older brother's fearlessness, found himself stuck and unable to retreat. John came to the rescue. With a foot on the windowsill and a hand on the casing, he stretched an arm upward while encouraging David to stretch a leg downward until the two met. "After securing a good hold, I jumped inside and dragged him in by his heels. This finished scootcher-scrambling for the night and frightened us into bed."

That rooftop event also foreshadowed a similar rescue on an Alaskan mountain in the summer of 1879.

Muir had taken passage on a mail boat to reach the north

country to satisfy a longing to see the great glaciers there—a longing that would outlast seven such visits. During a layover along the coast of British Columbia, he announced his intention to climb Glenora Peak, intending to reach the summit by sunset and hurry back down in the dark. S. Hall Young, a Presbyterian missionary recently graduated from college and assigned to minister to the Indians of southeastern Alaska, convinced Muir to take him along. Time for the climb was short, and the explorers hiked swiftly until reaching the higher pinnacles when, according to Young, "Muir began to *slide* up the mountain. I had been with mountain climbers before, but never one like him." Muir, Young said, had "a sure instinct for the easiest way into a rocky fortress, an instant and unerring attack, a serpent-like glide up the steep."

Young first found himself challenged to keep up, then unable to. Several yards ahead, Muir called back to warn Young of a particularly difficult spot and was startled a few seconds later by a cry for help. He rushed down the back trail and found Young clinging desperately to tenuous handholds while both legs hung dangerously over the edge and into a thousand feet of empty air. Muir disappeared, then reappeared on a narrow lip on the cliff below Young, from where he could barely reach one dangling foot. He reassured his companion that there was no danger and urged Young to slip over the edge as Muir supported him and guided his descent onto the shelf.

But that did not solve the problem. Both of Young's shoulders were dislocated, rendering his arms useless. Muir scuffed out footholds to guide his friend's steps, then lifted, hoisted, and rolled him to a safer place, and there tried to snap the joints back into place. After a good deal of painful twisting and turning and tugging, the job was half accomplished—one shoulder was wrenched back into its socket; the other refused to budge.

The two men spent a long, cold night inching down the mountain, with Muir alternately leading and lifting his young charge by whatever means he could devise. They stopped frequently along the way to rest and warm themselves by brief fires Muir kindled, making it back to the boat long past sunrise.

The ocean voyage that carried Muir from the Old World to the New reveals yet more of the man to come. Eleven-year-old John and several members of his family emigrated from Scotland in 1849, in a stormy Atlantic crossing that kept most of the passengers huddled belowdecks, heaving with seasickness and seeking shelter from the wind. Muir, however, spent the days "rejoicing in sympathy with the big curly-topped waves" and watching the sailors at their work, learning their ropes and knots and sails and songs. This fascination with nature's spectacular violence stayed with him throughout his life, evidenced by his glorious, gushing accounts in praise of storms of wind, of rain, of lightning, of snow, even earthquakes and avalanches.

His incessant curiosity persisted. Everything in nature seemed to fascinate him, boy and man. He would spend hours propped against a tree trunk watching the changing play of light on forest and mountain. He thought nothing of sitting in the summer sun as still as stone beside a trail to determine which small creature was responsible for a lacy pattern of tracks in the sand. Many a pleasant afternoon was spent studying the petals of an unfamiliar flower or a patch of moss clinging to rocky crag.

Determination, tenacity, and sacrifice were other lifelong

qualities Muir developed in his youth, qualities that seemed to emerge during his years in Wisconsin. His father had determined to settle there among Scotsmen with similar religious inclinations. With dark-to-dark labor provided mainly by the children, the family carved Fountain Lake Farm out of the wilderness near the village of Kingston, about seventy miles northwest of the thriving metropolis of Milwaukee.

A relatively well-to-do grain merchant in Scotland, Daniel Muir was unaccustomed to hard, physical labor. His personal preference was for a sedentary life studying scripture. His reading of the text did not temper his belief that children would somehow benefit from working themselves into a state of exhaustion six long days every week, so he loaded most of the burden of clearing land and running the farm on boys and girls alike. The family patriarch no doubt worked on occasion, as John wrote of him hauling lumber and attempting other tasks. Mostly, though, religious fanaticism drove father Muir to devote his energy to Bible study, itinerant preaching, and enforcing among his children strict rules of conduct, in full harmony with biblical imperative, by not sparing the rod.

The lake on the homestead proved irresistible as a swimming hole to the Muir boys and others who lived nearby, and they spent many a Sunday afternoon following church services—the Sabbath being their only day of rest from farmwork—splashing, diving, fishing, and rowing. The boys learned to swim on their own, following their father's advice that the frogs "will give you all the lessons you need."

Learning through trial and error to swim both above and below the surface and to hold his breath for long periods, John decided he was due an attempt at deeper water. He swam out to the deepest part of the lake—twenty or thirty feet deep—where a pair of neighbor boys were fishing in a skiff. He intended to surprise them by sneaking up on them and rocking the boat. He paddled quietly into position behind the boat and raised his arms to grab the stern, not realizing that the motion would push him underwater. He made it back to the surface but thrashed around in fear and panic, which resulted in continued dunkings. The boys in the boat thought he was only joking, so they did not pull him out until he had nearly drowned.

"I was very much ashamed of myself," he remembered, but decided that "unmanly fear" was a sorry excuse for failure, so soon after he returned to the scene of his disgrace. "I rowed directly out to the middle of the lake," he wrote, "stripped, stood up on the seat in the stern, and with grim deliberation took a header and dove straight down." Over and over he repeated the exercise, diving deep and stroking his way to the surface, then paddling round and round the skiff, building confidence. "Never was a victory over self more complete," he said. "I have been a good swimmer ever since."

By 1857, Daniel Muir's abusive farming practices—overworking the soil, failing to rotate crops and keep the fields properly manured—had reduced the productivity of Fountain Lake Farm, and he determined to move on, claiming a new homestead some five miles farther into the receding wilderness. This one he christened Hickory Hill, and once again John, the oldest son at nineteen years of age, was given the hardest of the work of clearing fields, breaking ground, and putting up fences and buildings. Perched on a hilltop, the home site lacked a ready water supply so the young man was told to dig until he found one.

The first ten feet—of ninety that would prove necessary for a reliable well—were shoveled up without incident, but then he hit solid sandstone. An attempt was made to break up the rock by blasting, but the senior Muir lacked skill or experience with explosives and the effort failed.

John was handed a heavy hammer and a set of mason's chisels and spent the coming days and weeks and months cramped in the bottom of a hole three feet wide chipping away with grim determination. From first light until last, he broke rock, his only respite coming at midday when his father or a brother hoisted up the fruits of his labor—a bucketful of fragmented sandstone—then lowered the bucket again to haul him out for dinner.

When the hole reached eighty feet deep it nearly killed him. After being lowered one morning, Muir was overcome by "choke-damp," deadly gases that had settled in the bottom overnight. After a time, realizing that his son was not loading the bucket with yesterday's sandstone chips, his father yelled down the hole. The noise startled John out of his lethargy, and he feebly called back a request to be taken out, which was accomplished after a few unsuccessful attempts to cling to the rope.

A miner who lived nearby was consulted about the incident and told Muir and his family, "Many a companion of mine have I seen dead with choke-damp, but none that I ever saw or heard of was so near to death in it as you were."

The miner showed the Muirs how to clear out the gas by throwing water down the shaft, and by forcing the deadly air up out of the hole by pushing fresh air down it with a plunger made from a bundle of brush or hay tied at the end of a rope.

After the near-fatal incident, John returned to the hole and chipped out another ten feet a hammer blow at a time. He eventually unearthed what he called "a fine, hearty gush of water . . . from which we all drank for many a day."

As man and boy, Muir had an unquenchable thirst for knowledge; he wanted to know everything, to understand everything, to comprehend the whys and hows and what-ifs of everything. He devoured books when given the chance, but books were scarce in his youth. Novels, certainly, and most other books save the Bible were banned in the Muir household as frivolous distractions, so he read the Bible, from his days in Scotland on, learning by heart the whole of the New Testament and three-fourths of the Old. Borrowed books, and the occasional volume he could obtain for himself, were treasured and studied almost as thoroughly whenever an opportunity presented itself.

When Muir was seventeen, he was found reading one evening a few minutes past the family's eight o'clock bedtime. Although he protested, he was told by his stern father that he could not stay up late with a book. The father relented somewhat, however, and said the boy would be allowed to arise as early as he liked, and read before his daily duties. Since he was more than willing to sacrifice sleeping for reading, and despite a body wearied by a long day of hard labor, Muir bounded from bed early the next morning—one o'clock, as it turned out—and hurried down to the kitchen to return to his book.

But Wisconsin winters make for a cold house, especially one in which no morning fire was permitted until time for breakfast cooking, and his feeble candle offered little in the way of warmth. Still, considering his newfound freedom exhilarating, he opted to spend the wee hours in the cellar trying to bring to life some of the mechanical plans and designs that filled his head.

Night after night, he tinkered. He sawed and whittled, cut and shaped, built and rebuilt, tested and tried, proved and improved. The results were as ingenious as they were well-crafted—a miniature but fully functional sawmill, water-wheels, latches and locks, thermometers, barometers, pyrometers, automatic devices to light lamps and strike fires, even a machine for feeding horses.

And clocks. Clocks of sundry sizes and shapes, clocks that told the day, week, and month as well as the hour; and, ultimately, an intricate clock-driven bedstead contraption he called an "early-rising machine." At a preset time, it tipped the bed frame to awake the occupant and stand him upon his feet.

The results of Muir's sacrificed sleep would eventually take him to the Wisconsin State Agricultural Society Fair, his first step out of his father's house and into a life of his own, and the first opportunity to put all the lessons of his youth to the test.

Practical Man, Impractical Life

Americans tend to admire the useful, the functional, the pragmatic, the practical. (As Poor Richard told the colonists in his *Almanack,* "There's many witty men whose brains can't fill their bellies.") Americans also like action, and prefer that action to lead to observable results, and these more often than not, measurable in terms of money.

At times in his life, John Muir floated in those mainstream American waters. Far from the stereotype of an impractical dreamer, he out-paddled most, reached shore more quickly, and his nets hauled in a bigger catch. On those occasions when he turned his hand to industry and agriculture he invariably achieved success and earned the respect and admiration of company, coworkers, competitors, and customers. He also earned a good deal of money.

But Muir never was happy in such endeavors and took no satisfaction in such achievements. He much preferred an "impractical" way of life. He would rather seek knowledge for its own sake, not merely for its application; appreciate the intrinsic worth of nature rather than count its value in coin; look backward into deep time rather than set his sights on tomorrow; enjoy beauty on its own terms instead of modifying it for his own purposes; pursue what he perceived to be right in favor of what was expedient. These things he did deliberately, with eyes wide open.

His first independent venture outside the family fold occurred in 1860 when he was twenty-two years old. Following the encouragement of neighbors, he bundled up some of his handmade wooden clocks and other devices of his invention and craftsmanship, and set out with a hope of exhibiting them at the Wisconsin State Agricultural Society Fair in Madison. The very picture of a country bumpkin, he wore homemade clothes and already displayed the wild, tangled beard and tousled hair that would become lifelong trademarks. His manners were uncouth and his social skills unsophisticated. He was painfully shy.

Fair officials—particularly Jeanne Carr, who would become a lifelong friend, mentor, and influence—saw in his entries evidence of genius worthy of special recognition. Carr was the wife of Ezra Carr, a professor at the University of Wisconsin in Madison under whom Muir would later study, but it was with Jeanne Carr that the young man formed a special bond.

His collection of handcrafted clocks elaborately whittled from native wood, a handmade and extremely sensitive thermometer, and his "early-rising machine" were displayed in the fair's Fine Arts Hall, for lack of a better place to feature inventions that defied categorization. The novel entries drew an abundance of attention from fairgoers and the press. Young boys—one the son of Ezra and Jeanne Carr—lined up for chances to be "awakened" again and again by Muir's curious early-rising device, which, reliably and on schedule, tipped them giggling out of the bed and onto their feet amidst the awe and admiration of onlookers. The "Meritorious Inventions" earned him a citation reading, "The clocks presented by J. Muir exhibited great ingenuity. The Committee regard him as a genius in the best sense, and think the state should feel pride in encouraging him." A five-dollar prize accompanied the award.

More important to Muir, and part of his motivation in attending the fair, was the notice his devices received from other inventors and craftsmen. One such was Norman Wiard, inventor of a prizewinning boat designed to move across the ice of frozen rivers. Wiard offered the budding craftsman on-the-job training in mechanical drawing and foundry operations in exchange for his service as mechanic on the ice boat.

Muir accepted the offer over others more substantial and spent the winter on the shores of the Mississippi River in Prairie du Chien, a Wisconsin town that lies on a line running westward from Milwaukee through Madison and on to the river that forms the state's border with Iowa. But haphazard organization, a lack of challenging work, and a dearth of training or instruction caused the apprentice to become disillusioned with Wiard, his boat, and his lessons, and so in the spring of 1861 he returned to Madison. There he worked such odd jobs as he could find while trying to determine how to afford enrollment at the University of Wisconsin.

He learned from a student he chanced to meet that a

young man could attend the college inexpensively if willing to live on campus and do without such luxuries as regular meals. Muir enrolled. His brief and infrequent attendance at regular schools since arriving in America required participation in preparatory classes, but his professors soon found the self-taught young man more than adequately prepared for regular studies.

His selection of classes, however, was anything but regular. He said he avoided the prescribed and practical courses of study as outlined and "instead picked out what I thought would be most useful to me, particularly chemistry, which opened a new world, and mathematics and physics, a little Greek and Latin, botany and geology."

His room became a popular stopping place for students, professors, and visitors to the campus. Every shelf, sill, nook, cranny, and flat surface was cluttered with objects of every description—fresh-cut and dried plants, mineral specimens, and a miscellany of jars, jugs, tubes, and bottles both empty and filled with odd items of interest.

His penchant for peculiar inventions continued at college and was also in evidence in his quarters. Handcrafted wooden machines and contrivances were stacked and heaped about. There was a "loafer's chair," of his invention, which fired a startling blank charge from a pistol once its occupant relaxed enough to lean back in the seat. An intricately hand-carved study desk housed whittled cogs and gears and wheels that became animated at preset intervals to place an open book before the reader, then removed the book to replace it with the next. His early-rising machine was also present, but the early-morning bang of the tipping bed was too disruptive for daily life in the dormitory, so the invention became an unused object of curiosity.

Muir attended classes at the university with some regularity for more than two years, but was never listed as higher than a first-year student owing to his odd selection of courses. Records showed his class status as "irregular gent" and he never earned a graduation certificate. He did, however, gain knowledge, particularly in geology and botany, that would inform his wilderness wanderings in years to come.

During the winter of 1861–62, he gave up student life temporarily to teach and earn money for spring term tuition. He took a position in a country school in Oak Hill, Wisconsin, ten miles south of Madison and the university, and soon grew accustomed to facing students each day.

Among his duties was to rise early and kindle a fire in the schoolhouse stove to cut the bitter winter morning chill before the students arrived for class. To this simple but tedious chore, he applied his inventiveness and inclination to tinker. He would place a mixture of powdered chlorate of potash and sugar in the stove along with tinder and kindling, and rigged a handmade clock to add a measured drop of sulfuric acid to the potion at the appointed hour. Every day, all winter, his fire-starter worked reliably.

Muir could have continued teaching, but returned to the university for more studies until, a year later, his growing wanderlust and the increasing threat of the military draft sent him north to Canada. The drafts of 1862 and 1863 had passed him by, but with Lincoln's orders for another half million men in March 1864, he feared his luck would not hold.

He spent the Canadian spring, summer, and fall of 1864

wandering the woods and marshes surrounding Lake Huron "botanizing"—identifying and collecting plants. By late autumn, with funds running low and winter coming on, Muir met up with his younger brother Daniel in the town of Meaford, Ontario, and the two went to work at a sawmill and factory on the shores of the lake's Georgian Bay that turned out broom and pitchfork handles and wooden rakes. The mill owners utilized John's skills to both run the mill and build an addition to the factory, keeping him and his brother hard at work until the summer of 1865.

Since the war in the States had ended in the spring, Daniel returned to Wisconsin, but the mill owners convinced John to stay on. He agreed to do so only if allowed to go tramping around the woods during the warm months to continue his plant studies. Back on the job in the fall, he contracted with the mill owners to fill an order for thirty thousand broom handles on the condition that he be allowed to engineer improvements in the mill and factory. He worked tirelessly through the fall and early winter of 1865–66 on gadgets and inventions to improve the manufacturing process. He made the mill's self-feeding lathe more efficient, designed a machine to bore holes for rake teeth, another mechanism to set teeth in the holes, and designed and built other devices to automatically cut bows for rakes and bend and shape handles.

When the improved factory equipment was working to his satisfaction by February, Muir went to work to fill the order for broom handles. The astonished factory owners could scarcely believe the new manufacturing efficiencies. Once he started production, Muir turned out twenty-three thousand of the contracted broom handles in a single day.

As it turned out, while the broom handles were stacked for seasoning in every corner of the factory, fire broke out on March 1, 1866, and destroyed the building and all the work. He settled for a fraction of the money owed him under the contract (and most of that would not be collected for several years) and, at age twenty-eight, set out for the United States.

By studying maps, he chose Indianapolis, Indiana, as his destination. On paper, the city looked centrally located, had adequate railroad connections, and appeared large enough to house many factories where a man of his mechanical talents might find work. More important, the town had enough wild forest land surrounding it to satisfy his passion for botany.

His instincts proved correct, and soon after his arrival in the city in the spring of 1866, he found work running a circular saw in a carriage parts factory. By the end of his first week on the job he had proven his skill to his supervisors, and all the circular saws and their operators were placed under his charge. Within months, he was earning double wages as a reward for mechanical and time-saving improvements he suggested and implemented throughout the factory. He said in a letter to a sister, "Circumstances over which I have had no control almost compel me to abandon the profession of my choice, and take up the business of an inventor."

He continued to devise other machines and efficiencies for improved production of carriage wheels and wagon parts. He even completed a thorough time-and-motion study that improved profits for the firm and safety for the workers. When asked by friends if he intended to patent his inventions, Muir said, "all improvements and inventions ought to be the property of the human race. No inventor has the right to profit by an invention for which he deserves no credit. The idea of it was really inspired by the Almighty."

His employers were aware of Muir's attraction to the outdoors; he had even revealed to them his desire to wander away to South America in the tracks of the famed explorer Alexander von Humboldt. His purpose in working was simply to pocket enough money to pay for the trip. The company valued his services, however, and did its best to chain him to the job with increasing responsibility and generous compensation, eventually even offering him a partnership. Their efforts seemed to be paying off, and by the spring of 1867 he appeared to be firmly entrenched in the work of the factory, his dreams of traveling to the jungles of the Southern Hemisphere a distant hope, and even his wanderings in the Indiana woods were infrequent and unfulfilling. However, all that changed late in the night of March 6, 1867. While tightening heavy leather belts that carried power to the factory machines, a sharp tool Muir employed in the task slipped, its point embedding in his right eye. Not only did he lose sight in the injured eye, but in the left eye as well in "sympathetic shock." It was the doctor's opinion that the left eye would recover in time if given plenty of rest, but that he would remain blind in the other.

In a letter to his mother a few days later he wrote, "I am completely prostrated and the eye is lost. I have been confined to bed since the accident and for the first two or three days could not eat or drink a mouthful but I am a little better today and hope to be at work again in a month or two."

Upon learning of his accident and condition, Muir's friends in Madison, Wisconsin, Ezra and Jeanne Carr, arranged for an eye specialist to see the patient and that doctor had better news: the injured right eye, too, would partially recover, even though Muir would never see perfectly through it.

While following the prescribed treatment of lying for weeks in a dark room as his vision slowly returned and cleared, Muir took a hard look at his life and future. He feared he was becoming a slave to machines of his own devising and determined to invent a better life for himself. As he later explained it, "I could have become a millionaire, but I chose to become a tramp."

He started out on his first "tramp" the first day of September 1867, immediately upon recovery from the eye injury. Now twenty-nine years old, he left Indianapolis aboard a train that would take him south to the Ohio River, which he crossed into Louisville, Kentucky. His adventures from there are recorded in his book *A Thousand-Mile Walk to the Gulf*.

He had only a general sense of route and destination on setting out, claiming his plan was "simply to push on in a general southward direction by the wildest, leafiest, and least trodden way I could find, promising the greatest extent of virgin forest." Once he reached the Gulf of Mexico, he hoped to catch a ship to South America and continue his wanderings there.

Of the many observations he recorded on his thousand-mile walk, and of all the ideas he developed on the journey, one was most indicative of where his thoughts would take him in the future: "The world, we are told, was made especially for man—a presumption not supported by all the facts," he wrote. "A numerous class of men are painfully astonished whenever they find anything, living or dead, in all God's universe, which they cannot eat or render in some way what they call useful to themselves."

Equally telling was the opinion of a blacksmith Muir shared a meal with in the Cumberland Mountains: "You look a strong-minded man, and surely you are able to do something better than wander over the country and look at weeds and blossoms. These are hard times," the man said, "and real work is required of every man that is able. Picking up blossoms doesn't seem to be a man's work at all in any kind of times." Despite the advice, Muir managed to avoid "a man's work" for most, but not all, of the rest of his life.

Malaria infected him when he reached Florida's Gulf Coast, forcing him to abandon his South American plans. He spent a brief time in Cuba, where the malaria visited him again, then he sailed to New York to book passage to California, another of the places he yearned to explore.

"We reached San Francisco about the first of April, and I remained there only one day, before starting for Yosemite Valley," Muir wrote of his 1868 arrival in the Golden State. His destination, the Yosemite Valley, is a gorge cut deep into the Sierra Nevada range, nearly due east of San Francisco. The first white man to see the place was the famous mountain man Joseph Reddeford Walker, who stumbled upon Yosemite's north rim in October 1833, while leading a company of fur trappers. The Merced River flows along the valley's bottom, which is four thousand feet above sea level and roughly seven miles long and a mile wide. Sheer, silvery granite cliffs line the valley, rising abruptly from the floor to tower four thousand feet over a wonderland of thundering waterfalls, forests of evergreen and oak, lush meadows, wildlife afoot and on the wing, and impressive rock formations. Muir had written to a friend a year earlier, "I read a description of the Yosemite Valley last year, and have thought of it almost every day since." His initial visit lasted only eight days but its effect endured. He determined to return as soon as time and money would allow.

He worked at odd jobs—breaking horses on a ranch, harvesting crops, operating a ferry, shearing sheep, and, finally, herding sheep in the mountains surrounding Yosemite. Although he did not like tending sheep he appreciated the job for keeping him away from cities and allowing plenty of time for hiking and studying nature. It was during this period that his lasting fascination with Sierra glaciers took hold and his theories about them began to form.

In a letter written to a sister that summer, Muir commented on his carefree, if unconventional, way of life. "I know that I could under ordinary circumstances accumulate wealth and obtain a fair position in society," he said. "But I am sure that the mind of no truant schoolboy is more free and disengaged from all the grave plans and purposes and pursuits of ordinary orthodox life than mine."

The winter of 1869 found him unable to resist the lure of the valley any longer. He reentered Yosemite and found employment with James Hutchings, who kept a hotel there. Hutchings was the first man to realize the tourist potential of Yosemite and had, in fact, led the first commercial excursion to the valley in 1863. A forty-niner who failed to strike it rich in the goldfields, he had turned to journalism, intending to publish an illustrated magazine devoted to the wonders of California. He had heard tales of Yosemite and set out in June 1855, with a friend and an illustrator to find the place, which few white men had yet seen. They found it and spent five days taking notes and making sketches. His first monthly, published in July 1856, featured the valley and attracted widespread interest. The magazine was one of many of Hutchings's creations extolling Yosemite; in fact, he was likely the author of the unforgettable description of the place that had attracted John Muir.

Hutchings had purchased the Upper Hotel in the valley in 1863, and that is where Muir found him, and went to work for him as a laborer in November 1869.

At first, Muir boarded with the Hutchings family, but soon constructed a cabin along Yosemite Creek and moved in, lulled to sleep at night by the thunder of nearby Yosemite Falls. He put in order the sawmill Hutchings had lately installed but could not make work, and spent much of his time sawing lumber. Partitions were installed in the primitive hotel (the "rooms" previously divided only by hanging sheets), chicken coops were constructed, and livestock fed. The hired man was also put in charge of watching over the Hutchings family when James went to Washington, D.C., on business for the winter.

In his spare time, Muir hiked in and out of the gorge, reading the rocks for miles around, turning his amateur's knowledge of geology into a theory of massive glaciers cutting, grinding, and shaping the Yosemite Valley and Sierra landscape—a theory in opposition to that of professional geologists.

Muir worked for Hutchings off and on from 1869 through 1871, running the sawmill, improving the hotel and outbuildings, tending the stock, and, increasingly, guiding tourists through the Yosemite wonderland. His popularity as a guide, however, did not bode well for a continuing relationship with his employer, a jealous man who considered himself the resident expert on Yosemite and who saw his employee as a poseur. By the time the two parted company in 1871, Muir's frugal ways had allowed him to save enough of the money Hutchings paid him to support his Sierra excursions and other explorations for years to come, keeping "real life" at bay for the better part of a decade.

During these years of relatively carefree wandering, he met, in 1874, and married, on April 14, 1880, Louie Wanda Strentzel. Introduced to Muir at a chance meeting at mutual friend Jeanne Carr's home, Louie was the only child of John Strentzel. A Polish refugee trained in Hungarian universities in medicine, horticulture, and viticulture who had emigrated to Texas in 1840, Strentzel moved on to California in 1849 and took up farming near the town of Martinez, in the Alhambra Valley near the northeastern edge of San Francisco Bay. In the curious California fashion, the Strentzel place was called a "ranch," but in fact consisted of orchards and vineyards sprawling across 2,600 acres of the countryside. Twenty acres of the productive land were carved out and presented to the newlyweds as a wedding gift.

In the months following the wedding, Muir worked on his small plot and lent a hand working his father-in-law's property until the grapes were ripe in July, then set out on an expedition to hunt glaciers in Alaska.

The trip was brief but eventful, and one of his adventures became one of the most popular of his many stories, the tale of crossing a glacier with Stickeen—"a brave doggie," said the storyteller. The dog belonged to a traveling companion but had gravitated to Muir. When the explorer set out on the stormy morning of August 30, 1880, to investigate Taylor Glacier, west of Glacier Bay, Stickeen—named for an Alaskan Indian tribe—would not be left behind. Muir said they spent a long, cold day wandering among and wondering at "rills and streams outspread over the ice-land prairie . . . never ceasing to admire their lovely color and music as they glided and swirled in their blue crystal channels and potholes." He wrote of "a magnificent uproar of pinnacles and spires and upheaving, splashing wave-shaped masses, a crystal cataract incomparable."

As the day lengthened, the pair found themselves stranded on the ice. "It was now near five o'clock and I was about fifteen miles from camp," Muir said, "and I had to make haste to recross the glacier before dark, which would come on about eight o'clock." For two hours, man and dog hurried across the "grand crystal prairies," working their way around streams and potholes, leaping crevasses, and crawling across ice bridges atop the shifting glacier. Caught on an island of ice between two yawning crevasses, Muir and Stickeen ran back and forth along the edges of the cracks searching for a place to cross. The only possibility was a sagging ice bridge, "the very worst of the sliver bridges I had ever seen," Muir said. The sharp edge of the span had weathered down into a sagging curve across the forty-foot crevasse, but the worst thing was that each end of the ice bridge joined the sides of the chasm eight or ten feet below surface level. Seeing no alternative, he began cutting footholds while the nervous dog whimpered and whined in fear. After reaching the knife-edge of the sliver, he straddled it and inched along, knocking off the pointed top and creating a four-inch-wide path for the dog to follow. Once across, it took considerable encouragement to persuade the reluctant dog to attempt a crossing, but, "finally, in despair he hushed his cries, slid his little feet slowly down into my footsteps," Muir said, and "walked slowly and cautiously along the sliver as if holding his breath." Upon reaching the far slope, the dog studied the notched steps cut there then "whizzed" up the side. Stickeen then "ran and cried and barked and rolled about fairly hysterical in the sudden revulsion from the depth of despair to triumphant joy." They made it back to camp safely by ten o'clock. The story of Stickeen remains one of Muir's most popular, told to countless audiences over the years and widely published in various renditions.

After returning home from the adventure, he worked hard at the ranch through fall and winter, and in March a daughter, Annie Wanda, was born, deepening his commitment to settle down to a more conventional way of life and provide a living for his family. He attacked the job of tending the orchards and vineyards with a passion, working long hours. The life did not agree with him, however, and among the results of his labors were chronic nervous indigestion, a persistent hacking cough, and a loss of appetite that reduced his weight to a bony one hundred pounds.

Shortly after Annie Wanda's birth on March 25, 1881, Muir received a request to join an expedition to search for lost ships in the Arctic—two whalers and the *Jeanette*, an exploring vessel. He first refused, probably owing to a desire to stay near his new baby. His wife, however, thought a journey to colder climes might improve his health, and Muir himself believed that the germs responsible for most maladies could not survive in the frigid north. So, when the United States revenue cutter *Thomas Corwin* steamed out of San Francisco Bay on May 4, 1881, Muir had boarded as scientific observer.

The expedition navigated the Bering Strait, explored the Siberian coast, broke through the ice of the Arctic Ocean to visit Alaska's northern coast, and explored a number of ice-bound islands. The searchers found evidence of the fate of one of the lost whaling ships, but neither the second whaler nor the *Jeanette* were recovered.

Muir did recover his health, however, and by September 1881 had returned to the orchards and vineyards. With renewed energy, he went at the work with determination and vigor. In addition to tending his own plot, he took over management of the Strentzel ranch in its entirety. Always a profitable operation, the ranch had been something of a horticultural experiment station and playground for old Dr. Strentzel, so had never reached its financial potential. His son-in-law set out to remedy this by eliminating production of several fruits and reducing the number of varieties of others until the crop consisted of Bartlett pears, cherries, and three of the most popular varieties of grapes. Upon these he lavished more time, attention, care, and labor than competitors were willing to match.

He bargained hard with buyers, refusing to sell until he had his price, and profitably shipped tons of fruit across the country. His meticulous approach to the operation revealed itself in small ways, such as his obsession with shipping crates. He showed up early at the docks, earlier than any other farmers were willing to, and sifted through the stacks of fruit lugs to select only strong ones in good repair in which to pack and protect his produce—a trivial thing, perhaps, but indicative of the intensity with which Muir pursued his work.

For nearly a decade he kept up the pace, devoting long hours to make the ranch a success. Another child—Helen Lillian— was born to the Muirs on January 23, 1886, and John made a few halting attempts at writing. Mostly, though, he pursued a life of hard, physical labor that bore fruit both in horticultural production and in building a bank account. "I had more money than I thought I would ever need for my family or for all the expenses of travel and study," he wrote.

But the gain came at a cost, and as seemed usual in Muir's case, the price was his health. The physical labor and emo- tional stress associated with the job, as well, perhaps, as a spirit unsuited to a settled life, reduced the man to a shadow of him- self. "I'm degenerating into a machine for making money," he said.

Louie encouraged him to return as often as possible to the wilderness to regain his health and refresh his spirit. One such getaway occurred in July 1888, when he took time from his ranch labors to explore, hike, and climb in the Pacific North- west and the Cascade Range. A letter from Louie, which found the explorer in Seattle, Washington, encouraged him to give up the work of the ranch in favor of wilderness and literary pur- suits. "A ranch that needs and takes the sacrifice of a noble life, or work, ought to be flung away," she wrote. Of his travel and writing, she said, "There is nothing that has a right to be con- sidered beside this except the welfare of our children."

When he returned home, he lightened his workload with Louie's assistance by immediately leasing out most of the ranch, and in 1891 he rid himself of it altogether by recruiting

a Nebraska brother-in-law to come west and manage the remainder. Free of the day-to-day worries of ranch work, and
bolstered by the small fortune he had earned, Muir could afford
to devote the remainder of his life to another kind of work—
much of which, to him, seemed more like play.

Women

Lengthy periods of John Muir's life were spent outside the company of women. His extended trips into the wild were often solo journeys, sometimes with other trail-hardened, vigorous men. His male friends were many, and with some he maintained lengthy relationships. Yet he seems to have preferred the company of women, although this rarely included the rituals of courtship, for he remained a bachelor until age forty-two. Perhaps he sought the company of women because they were more attuned to his appreciation for the beauty of nature; maybe his mystical and spiritual inclinations were better understood and appreciated from a feminine point of view.

Whatever the reasons, he was attracted to women, and from all accounts the attraction was mutual. Sometimes described as handsome, Muir was of shorter-than-average height, claiming that too much hard work during his teenage years on the Wisconsin farms had stunted his growth. His frame was lean and sinewy, occasionally shrinking to an emaciated condition from overwork, illness, or because of a sparse diet while exploring. Even when food was abundant, he ate little, for he lacked interest in food as anything other than fuel. His hair was auburn, later gray-shot, then gray, and usually unkempt; his long beard tousled and untrimmed. Blue eyes—one slightly discolored by an industrial accident—were his most remarkable feature, described variously as bright, engaging, mischievous, sparkling, and piercing. Although shy by nature, once he became comfortable with his company Muir was an eager, often domineering conversationalist. Whether in conversation or correspondence, he willingly and freely discussed feelings and emotions, thoughts and ideas, hopes and fears. This openness, perhaps, drew women to him. In any event, letters indicate that such guilelessness lay at the heart of his closest and most lasting friendship, that with Jeanne Carr.

She was not Muir's only close female friend, however. Other women he shared extensive time and attention with included Emily Pelton, a young lady he met while working in Prairie du Chien, Wisconsin, in 1860, and with whom he considered marriage. Another was Elvira Hutchings, wife of James Hutchings, the hotel keeper who employed him in the Yosemite Valley in 1869–70 and again in 1871. They became warm friends during the cold winter when Muir kept watch over her and a young daughter while her husband was in the East on business. Their closeness, in fact, became the subject of gossip and contributed to friction between employer and employee.

About that same time, in 1870, the celebrity lecturer and writer Therese Yelverton made an extended visit to Yosemite. Attracted to the sawmill operator and hotel caretaker, she made careful notes of Muir's habits and mannerisms during their long talks, and from him drew inspiration for the thinly disguised character Kenmuir in her 1872 novel, *Zanita: A Tale of the Yo-Semite.*

A few Muir biographers claim he had intimate romantic relationships with some or all of these women. However, most who have studied his life doubt that the man's strong moral sense would have allowed any such dalliances, even had the stringent Victorian codes of decency and conduct of the day permitted them.

Older women, too, were lured by the man's magnetism. Something about Muir must have suggested he needed mothering, and several women over the years took it upon themselves to provide it: Jean Galloway, who lived on a neighboring Wisconsin farm; Emily Pelton's mother, Frances, who ran a boardinghouse in Prairie du Chien, Wisconsin; college professor Catharine Merrill—one of the first American women to achieve that distinction—watched over Muir in Indianapolis. As well, Mrs. A. G. Black, the wife of a Yosemite hotel owner, mothered him, and Clara McChesney of Oakland, California, befriended Muir while he was there in 1873–74 writing his "Studies in the Sierra" magazine series on glaciers.

Jeanne Carr, thirteen years his senior, fits somewhere between Muir's female contemporaries and those of the previous generation, and their bond was unique. From their first meeting in 1860, when he was twenty-two years old and she thirty-five, the two spent much time together and exchanged volumes of correspondence in a relationship that endured until her death in 1903.

They met at the Wisconsin State Agricultural Society Fair where the young man participated as an exhibitor and she as a member of the fair board. Like other fair officials and members of the press and public, Muir's craftsmanship astounded her. She also saw in the rough-hewn rustic an eagerness, curiosity, and intelligence that she believed, with proper direction and guidance, would take him far.

Her friendship with Muir flourished after he enrolled for classes at the University of Wisconsin in 1861, where he became a student and later a friend of her husband, Ezra, a professor there. He was often a guest in their home, where he tutored and tended the children and made use of the extensive family library. After he left the university and while working in Canada, they began corresponding. Her initial letter to him no longer exists but his reply, dated September 13, 1865, does. In it, he thanked her for recommending a book and asked her to thank the professor "for his kind remembrance of me, but still more for the good patience he had with so inept a scholar," before he answered her purpose in writing.

"You propose, Mrs. Carr, an exchange of thoughts, for which I thank you very sincerely. This will be a means of pleasure and improvement for which I could not have hoped ever to have been possessed of," he wrote, "but then here is the difficulty: I feel that I am altogether incapable of properly conducting a correspondence with one so much above me." She disagreed. For the next thirty years they exchanged letters. Botany, of course, was often a topic, given their mutual fascination with plants. Other subjects included books, art, religion, philosophy, career considerations, writing, family, and travel.

Always, she offered emotional support. For example, while he was in Indianapolis in 1867 recovering from the injury to his eye, she wrote, "I have often wondered what God was training you for. He gave you the eye within the eye, to see in all natural objects the realized ideas of His mind." She then told him not to despair about his future. "Do not be anxious about it. He will surely place you where your work is."

Her advice and assistance extended to more practical matters as well. She continually encouraged Muir to write articles, essays, and books recording his ideas and adventures—even nagging him, when she thought it necessary—to take up the pen. It is likely he would never have been published were it not for her influence, both with him and with editors of her acquaintance. She even acted as a literary agent of sorts, often advising him on what and where to publish, occasionally handling negotiations and other arrangements, and always promoting his work to numerous publications and publishers.

In 1868, not long after Muir first arrived in California, Ezra Carr was dismissed from the University of Wisconsin over academic disagreements. In 1869 he accepted a position as professor of agriculture, chemistry, and horticulture at the newly created University of California in Oakland, which soon relocated to Berkeley, and the family followed. The proximity to Muir led Jeanne Carr to attempt greater control over his activities, and she often tried to talk him down from the mountains to meet and mingle with people she believed could help his budding literary career or otherwise prove beneficial in his life. Since it was difficult to get him to come down, she sometimes sent people up the mountain to him, among them the artist William Keith, University of California professor Joseph LeConte, Harvard scientist Asa Gray, even the famous Transcendentalist philosopher Ralph Waldo Emerson.

Their correspondence continued when Carr moved to Pasadena in 1880. There she wrote her last letter to him. While undated, it was probably written in 1895 and encouraged him, as she had done so often, to meet someone she thought worth knowing. She wanted him to call on a young woman traveling through San Francisco, a photographer formerly from Madison, Wisconsin, where both Carr and Muir had lived and where they had met. Photographs the woman had made of Muir Glacier in Alaska impressed Carr, as did the photographer. "She is bright, responsive, and an excellent raconteur," she wrote, then closed the letter with, "I rejoice in all that gives you honor and happiness, and am always, Yours faithfully, Jeanne Carr."

Muir's old friend died December 14, 1903, near Paso Robles, California, where her last days were spent in the care of relatives. Of the scores of letters they had exchanged over the years, one, which probably affected his life more than any other, had been written to someone else—an 1872 message to a young woman named Louie Wanda Strentzel. "I want you to know my John Muir," Carr wrote. "I wish I could give him to some noble young woman 'for keeps' and so take him out of the wilderness into the society of his peers." Carr hoped Louie would take on the task, and in 1874 she introduced them when the Strentzels and Muir happened to visit her home at the same time. Afterward, she encouraged the couple through their long acquaintance and lengthy courtship, until they finally became engaged in 1879 and married in 1880.

It was not a typical courtship. If John and Louie were impressed with one another on their initial meeting, they revealed no evidence of it. In fact, they had no further contact until late autumn 1877, when Muir arrived unannounced at the Strentzel ranch following a two-hundred-fifty-mile, two-week trip down the Merced and San Joaquin Rivers from Hopeton in the Sierra to Martinez near San Francisco Bay. He made the voyage in a porous little boat he said he built "out of some gnarled, sun-twisted fencing." Although unannounced, his visit was not uninvited—Louie's father, Dr. John Strentzel, had invited the traveler to visit the ranch when they had met at Carr's home three years before.

Two weeks afloat had left the explorer in sorry shape. His hair and beard were even wilder than usual, his frame emaciated. His clothing showed the wear and tear of wilderness living, and climbing out of the boat into the river to drag it across sandbars and through snags. Even so, the family welcomed him, he said, and attempted to fatten him up "with turkey, chicken, beef, fruits, and jellies in the most extravagant manner."

During the winter and spring months of early 1878 he made several trips from San Francisco, where he was at work writing, to the ranch. While a genuine friendship had developed with old Dr. Strentzel, Muir also spent much time walking and talking with Louie and it is likely that she was the real object of his visits.

Summer took him across the Sierra to the basin and range country of Nevada on an expedition for the United States Coast and Geodetic Survey. While away, he wrote frequently to the Strentzels, passing along news of his discoveries and adventures, including finding evidence of historical glaciers. He also told them of a near-fatal incident in which Muir and his companions almost perished from lack of water while high on a desert mountain.

The adventurer returned to San Francisco in the fall to continue writing, and resumed his habit of visiting Louie and her family frequently. Not until June 1879, however, would he finally propose marriage. She accepted. Her parents were delighted, as the next day's entry in her mother's diary attests: "Mr. Muir is the only man that the Dr. and I have ever felt we could take into our family as one of us and he is the only one that Louie has ever loved."

Louie's want for love had not been from lack of opportunity, however. Her wide gray eyes, framed in an oval face by dark hair and high, sculpted cheekbones made a pleasing picture. Much more than physical appearance, however, would have made her an attractive companion. The only child of a wealthy landowner, she had been well educated at a local college and was a skilled pianist many thought worthy of the concert stage. She was a shy girl, however, and showed little interest in the social whirl, turning down courtship and marriage proposals in favor of a quiet life at home with her family. Her scrupulous record keeping, which tracked the production of dozens of varieties of experimental fruit trees and grape vines, assisted with ranch management; she also helped her mother manage the household. She grew so content with the security of life at home that customary marriageable age passed her by, and she was thirty-two when she accepted the proposal of the forty-one-year old Muir.

Their betrothal went unannounced. The groom-to-be had

made plans to embark on the first of what would be many expeditions to Alaska and they decided to keep the engagement secret until his return. Despite his closeness to Jeanne Carr and the plotting on her part that led to the proposal, Muir's June 19, 1879 letter to her announcing his departure the next day for a "summer in the snow and ice and forests of the north coast" does not even hint at his new status as a failing bachelor. Moreover, the friendship of the senior Strentzels with Carr did not include informing her of either the engagement or the wedding. In a May 1880 letter to Mrs. Strentzel, Carr tells how she "read the news in Wednesday's *Record Union*—just a week after the wedding." She was delighted with the development. "I am grateful to you all that you have enclosed with love one so precious to me," she wrote of her friend Muir. "It seems a suitable mating and rarely do two spirits so finely tuned strike the perfect chord." Still, she wanted more. "I shall be interested in every particular which any of you may care to repeat to me."

Muir had returned to the States from Alaska in early January 1880, but agreed to stay in Portland, Oregon, for a time to deliver lectures, then stayed over in San Francisco on business. In mid-February, after eight months away, he came home to the Strentzel ranch and within two months found himself a married man with new and unaccustomed responsibilities.

The marriage was unconventional. The newlyweds were much older than the norm and perhaps beyond youthful expectations of passionate romance. Although he would write volumes on a variety of topics during his life, Muir wrote very little about Louie or their relationship, and, from all accounts, seldom spoke of her even among friends. She was equally quiet about the marriage, leaving no written accounts of her life or their life together. They made an odd couple, even a poor match in many ways. While both were shy in the company of strangers, he became gregarious as he grew acquainted, while she remained reticent. She was fastidious and proper; he cared little for appearances or social customs. He was restless and always longed to be on the move; she was a homebody. She was submissive; his personality was forceful and domineering. Yet it seems that he changed his ways more dramatically than she in order to accommodate the partnership, and between them they made a comfortable relationship that lasted for life.

The wedding gift from the Strentzels of a house and twenty acres of productive orchards gave the union the advantage of a firm financial foundation. Muir immediately set out to improve their holdings, determined to accumulate sufficient wealth to keep his wife and the children they expected comfortable. After brief trips to Alaska in 1880 and 1881 he gave up his wanderings and stayed close to home for the next several years.

In addition to the twenty acres the couple owned, Muir leased more land and soon had the responsibility of managing the entire Strentzel estate. Hard work earned him profitability and wealth, but also exhaustion and poor health. His obsession with the orchards and vineyards troubled Louie, concerned both with his failing health and the neglect of his writing career. Acting as cajoler, critic, and editor, she encouraged him to keep at his craft, carefully managing household activities to provide the peace and quiet he required for writing, even having the music room soundproofed so the piano would not disturb him. He doted on the two "bairns"—the Scots term for children—born to the marriage, Annie Wanda and Helen Lillian, and as they grew he revealed the glories of nature to them on walks through the orchards and filled their young ears with stories of his travels and adventures.

His lingering illnesses—coughing, unsettled stomach, loss of appetite—continued to worry Louie as his body withered and his disposition worsened, and she urged him to get back to the mountains and woods he loved. He took her advice only when she could convince him the fruit trees and vines would allow a brief absence. In July 1884 she demanded a vacation herself and insisted he escort her to Yosemite, more for his benefit than hers as she did not enjoy being away from home and its comforts. When an 1885 premonition of his father's forthcoming death sent him eastward, she suggested he make it an extended visit, which he did, detouring through the Mount Shasta region in Northern California and Yellowstone Park in Wyoming Territory.

Louie finally persuaded him, in 1888, that fruit growing, though lucrative, was not worth the cost to his health or his literary duties. She offered firm, but gentle, direction in a letter that would again change the course of his life. His ranch work "ought to be flung away beyond all reach and power for harm," she wrote. As long as the children were provided for—which they were—the fruit trees and grape vines were not worth "the sacrifice of a noble life and work." Convinced, he turned the orchards and vineyards over to others and resumed the less conventional but more fulfilling course he had abandoned a decade earlier.

As Muir's travels in the years to come took him further

afield for longer periods, Louie maintained the home place and provided stability for their daughters. Helen Lillian was a frail and sickly child, often stricken with bouts of pneumonia. By May 1905, worry over her condition led Muir to follow a doctor's advice to a drier climate in order to save his daughter's life. Annie Wanda, the older girl, accompanied them, and father and daughters set up camp in the fresh, open air of the desert near Willcox, Arizona while mother stayed at home in Martinez.

They had barely settled in when a telegram arrived from California, dated June 24, calling Muir home. Louie was dangerously ill. The diagnosis was lung cancer and the prognosis grave. She died August 6, 1905. Lacking the will for any other course of action, the widower packed up his grief and returned to Arizona, this time to the Painted Desert.

Thus ended a contented, if unconventional, marriage. Over the years, the partners developed a deep and abiding affection that sustained them through extended periods apart, as well as their time together. Muir's willingness to set aside his wanderlust and lead a more orthodox life, at least for a time, is evidence of his commitment to the union. Louie's appreciation for her husband's calling, her acceptance of his eccentricities, and her willingness not only to accommodate but encourage him, more than balanced the scales. Theirs proved to be, as Jeanne Carr predicted, "a suitable mating."

The other women in the family, Annie Wanda and Helen Lillian, married and produced a "boy undergrowth" that delighted Muir in his seniority. At the time of his death, Annie Wanda Muir Hanna still lived at the old Strentzel ranch in Martinez with her husband Mark, a civil engineer, and their four sons. Helen Lillian Muir married Buel Funk, a cattle rancher, and lived on a ranch at Daggett, near Barstow in Southern California's Mojave Desert. The birth of their third son prompted Muir's final journey—a trip to the ranch to introduce himself to his newest grandchild.

The Mystic

The physical world was very much John Muir's home. He lived intimately with its rocks and trees, flowers and mountains, waterfalls and glaciers. At the same time, he lived with an awareness of another world, a place of spirituality and mysticism he found always nearby, often present, and occasionally overwhelming.

His religious journey started early in life. Strict observance of a stringent ideology was ever in demand in the family home. Patriarch Daniel Muir held to an unforgiving interpretation of a Scotch Calvinist brand of Christianity. That creed frowned on frivolity (and held most things as frivolous) and viewed mankind as depraved creatures destined to and deserving of a harsh existence in which joy had no place. Ranging from zealotry to fanaticism, he often thundered from the pulpit as a lay minister, and after immigrating to Wisconsin in 1849 habitually traveled throughout the region to preach at worship services and revivals. On one occasion, he drove a horse to ruin in order to reach a religious gathering on time. The horse never recovered, and the Muir children, to whom it belonged as a pet, watched it die.

Devoting most of his time and attention to Bible study, Daniel put the burden on his children to make the family homestead into a productive farm, and, as the oldest son, John bore the heaviest load. On top of hard physical labor, the Muir children were forced to study the Bible continually and to commit long passages to memory under threat of punishment. They were also required to sit in silence for hours as their father preached or prayed on Sabbath mornings, whether at home or at church.

If this strict upbringing was meant to indoctrinate the Muir children to their father's mode of belief, it failed, at least in John's case. The more he learned of the Bible, the more it taught him to disagree with his father's interpretations. Where Daniel was drawn to hard, demanding, severe teachings mined from the Old Testament, John's natural inclination was to the gentler, more loving approach preached in the Gospels of the New Testament. Where Daniel saw the natural world as a dreary place existing solely for man's dominion, John saw beauty, and in that beauty, evidence of God's love. He came to see, as well, a connectedness among all life, and mankind as but one strand in a web of God's creations.

His views often clashed with those of his father, these disagreements usually resulting in discipline or punishment. On occasion, however, young John used the very scriptures his father revered to temper the man's demands on the family. For example, Daniel Muir joined many across the country in following a fad diet introduced by Sylvester Graham, a Presbyterian minister from Massachusetts for whom the graham cracker is named. Otherwise largely forgotten today, Graham published a popular two-volume text promoting his nutritional theories in 1839 and lectured widely on the subject until his death in 1851. He blamed meat for a variety of ills ranging from stimulating carnal appetites to alcoholism to a sallow complexion. His dietary plan limited food intake to fruits and vegetables and above all bread baked from "graham flour," a coarsely ground, unsifted flour that contained the entire wheat kernel including the bran. When Daniel Muir put the family under the meatless nutritional regimen and supported his actions with scripture, John successfully countered with the story from the Old Testament's First Book of Kings in which the Lord sent ravens with bread *and* flesh to feed the prophet Elijah.

Once on his own and outside the sphere of his father's direct influence, Muir's religious views would continue to evolve in a divergent direction, but the weight of his father's teaching was neither easily nor quickly set aside. While studying at the University of Wisconsin in Madison in 1861 and 1862, for example, he often visited and preached uninvited sermons to Union soldiers billeted at the state fairgrounds, badgering them to avoid temptation and live the Christian life, never forgetting the final judgment that awaits all. He was known around campus, too, as overly fervent in his religious views and too eager to share them with others, even to the point of attempting to correct behavior in others he considered improper. Still later, during his two-year sojourn in Canada in 1864–66, religious disagreements with his employers were among his reasons for leaving the job at a sawmill and manufacturing plant to return to the United States.

During his thousand-mile walk through several Southern states in 1867, Muir's developing religious ethic took large strides. In his writings from the trip, he observed that in relating to nature, men tend to be "selfish, conceited creatures . . . blind to the rights of all the rest of creation." Responding to comments he heard in the swamps of Florida that alligators must be beasts built by the devil, he wrote, "Fierce and cruel they appear to us, but beautiful in the eyes of God. They, also are His children," and, "Though alligators, snakes, etc., naturally repel us, they are not mysterious evils. They dwell happily in these flowery wilds, are part of God's family, unfallen, undepraved, and cared for with the same species of tenderness and love as is bestowed on angels in heaven or saints on earth." Extending the theme, he wrote that God's creation would be "incomplete without the smallest transmicroscopic creature that dwells beyond our conceitful eyes and knowledge."

Muir always considered himself an adherent of the Christian religion, but his was a personal form of Christianity often at odds with the more conventional and orthodox sects of his time. His beliefs drifted toward pantheism but while he never fully accepted that philosophy, which holds that God and nature are one and the same, that neither exists apart from the other, he did believe the spirit of the Creator existed in all of nature and wrote that with the same dust of the earth from which God fashioned man, He "made every other creature, however noxious and insignificant to us. They are earth-born companions and our fellow mortals. . . . Plants are credited with but dim and uncertain sensation, and minerals with none at all. But why may not even a mineral arrangement of matter be endowed with sensation of a kind that we in our blind exclusive perfection can have no manner of communication with?"

While he said that man and nature had "no manner of communication," other writings show he thought otherwise. He came to believe that communing with wild nature could restore and refresh the spirit, a cleansing and a renewal not unlike the Christian rite of baptism, an analogy he made many times in his writings. An example of this idea is found in his essay describing Twenty Hill Hollow, a valley located in Merced County on California's central plain. "Hide in the hills of the Hollow, lave in its waters, tan in its golds, bask in its flower-shine, and your baptisms make you a new creature indeed," he wrote. "Or, choked with the sediments of society, so tired of the world, here will your hard doubts disappear, your carnal incrustations melt off, and your soul breathe deep and free in God's shoreless atmosphere of beauty and love." He concluded the essay: "You bathe in these spirit-beams, turning round and round, as if warming at a camp-fire. Presently you lose consciousness of your own separate existence: you blend with the landscape, and become part and parcel of nature."

Muir came to believe, too, in a personal mission to baptize, a mission akin to that of the biblical John the Baptist, who, Muir said, "was not more eager to get all his fellow sinners into the Jordan than I to baptize all of mine in the beauty of God's mountains."

The mystical mountaineer once baptized himself, without intending to, in the deluge of Upper Yosemite Falls, which, with a drop of 1,430 feet, is the world's highest free-falling waterfall. Plunging down the sheer granite walls that line the Yosemite

Valley in California's central Sierra Nevada range, the upper falls are connected by a tumbling cascade to the Lower Yosemite Falls. The lower waterfall seems almost insignificant in the grandeur of the deep gorge, yet with a drop of 320 feet, it is more than twice the height of the more celebrated Niagara Falls.

Muir's drenching took place in the light of the moon on April 3, 1871, when he scaled the cliffs to see the Yosemite Valley in pale light filtered through the upper falls, and to view lunar rainbows that sometime appear in its mists. Deciding to see the valley from the very perspective of the fall itself, he inched along a narrow ledge until he huddled against the rock behind the vertical stream. Then, a shift in the wind resulted in tons of water crashing down on him as he clung desperately to his thin granite perch. "Down came a dash of spent comets, thin and harmless-looking in the distance," he wrote, "but they felt desperately solid and stony when they struck my shoulders, like a mixture of choking spray and gravel, and big hailstones."

He took the opportunity offered by another shift of the wind to move a few feet along the ledge and wedge himself behind an ice block, clinging there until he felt it safe to crawl away from Yosemite Falls altogether. Even in this narrow escape, inches away from being swept to his death, Muir found glory. A letter to a friend relating the experience claimed that when it comes to the relationship to stone and stream, men know little of the "profound attractions and repulsions of our spiritual affinities!" He summed up his visit to the "spirit of this rock and water": "How significant does every atom of our world become amid the influences of those beings unseen, spiritual, angelic mountaineers that so throng these pure mansions of crystal foam and purple granite."

A few years earlier, during his first visit to the Yosemite Valley in 1868, Yosemite Falls was the setting for another of Muir's encounters with "spiritual, angelic mountaineers" of a more supernatural kind. This time, he was on the canyon's edge above the falls, trying to see how it looked from above. Creeping down the steep ledge on hands, feet, and backside toward the waterfall's verge, the view from each new vantage point he reached was blocked by another irregularity in the surface of the granite. A study of the rock revealed a narrow lip a little farther down, upon which he believed he could rest his heels. Following the narrow shelf horizontally for a few yards brought him to the brink of the waterfall and a "perfectly free view down into the heart of the snowy, chanting throng of comet-like streamers into which the fall soon separates." Even in his precarious position Muir felt protected, claiming he was "not distinctly conscious of danger" and that the splendor "at close range, smothered the sense of fear, and in such places one's body takes keen care for safety on its own account." Lost in the moment, all sense of time escaped him and he could not say how long he clung there or even by what power he returned from his precipitous perch.

Another example of this strange sense of protection linked to a supernatural "other self" occurred in 1872 on a sheer cliff near the summit of Mount Ritter, a 13,300-foot peak in the Sierra Nevada range. Rugged in the extreme, ringed by glacier and gorge, the summit was considered inaccessible by many. "But difficulties of this kind," Muir said, "only exhilarate the mountaineer." He carefully scrutinized the mountain's upper reaches to map out the route for his solo climb. Even so, he found himself at a halt on a vertical rock face, clinging desperately with outstretched hands and feet, unable to proceed up, down, or sideways, and fearing he was doomed to fall. Soon, however, Muir said he "seemed suddenly to become possessed of a new sense. The other self—the ghost of by-gone experiences, Instinct, or Guardian Angel—call it what you will—came forward and assumed control." In this trance of extremely acute perception, finger- and footholds revealed themselves and he made his way up the cliff to the relative safety of the summit. "Had I been borne aloft upon wings, my deliverance could not have been more complete," he said.

Strange though such occurrences may have seemed to others, Muir did not hesitate to use a claim of uncanny protection to his advantage on at least one occasion. This occurred in Alaska in 1879 during his first expedition to study the glaciers there. Muir, though an amateur, was considered by then something of an expert on glaciers based upon his studies of them in the Sierra Nevada. Among other accomplishments during his initial tour of Alaska, he was credited as the first white man to discover Glacier Bay. Several giant glaciers meet the sea in the bay, located where the southern arm of Alaska tucks under its border with British Columbia. Even though Indians in the area claimed it had already been visited by Russians, and that other seal hunters had seen the place, it was Muir's discovery that stuck, and the names of most of its glaciers are the ones he gave them.

The discovery almost never happened, though, as some of the Indians guiding Muir on the nearly eight-hundred-mile canoe voyage grew concerned over stormy weather and the lateness of the season, and refused to enter the bay for fear of being trapped by icebergs calving from the many glaciers that feed the bay. "I made haste to reassure them," Muir said, "telling them that for ten years I had wandered alone among mountains and storms, and that good luck always followed me; that with me, therefore, they need fear nothing." He told them that "Heaven cared for us, and guided us all the time," but that "only brave men had a right to look for heaven's care, therefore all childish fear must be put away." The Indians believed him.

Still another mystical aspect of Muir's life was an occasional and unusual prescience of current or future events that sometimes overwhelmed him. The first of these telepathic experiences, at least the first he recorded, was the sudden unexpected knowledge that an old friend was nearby. While watching over a herd of sheep grazing atop the north wall of Yosemite Valley in early August 1869, Muir felt—knew— that Professor James Davie Butler, who had taught him Latin and the classics at the University of Wisconsin, was in the valley below. It is necessary to note that Butler had written to his former student that he might—*might*—travel to Yosemite that summer but did not know when, or even if. So when awareness of the professor's presence struck Muir, the surprise of it prompted him to scramble down a canyon toward the valley. When he realized he could not outrun the approaching night, he opted to return to the sheep camp and make his descent in the morning. He struck out at first light, but missed Butler at the hotel—although he did verify his presence in Yosemite from the register. Muir soon overtook the hiking professor, who, like his finder, was astonished to be found under those circumstances.

Another such occurrence came in a sadder situation, but the telepathy involved was more remarkable in that it happened across a much greater distance than those few miles from the north rim to the floor of Yosemite Valley. While writing in his study one late August day in 1885, Muir was filled with a premonition of his father's death. Ironically, his last contact with his father had been more than ten years before when, in a letter, the senior Muir advised his son that the best thing to do with the book he was working on was to "burn it and then it will do no more harm either to you or to others." In any event, the son not only believed the mystical presentiment of his father's approaching death, he convinced several of his brothers and sisters of its veracity. It took Muir more than a month to gather his siblings and reach Kansas City, where his ailing father was living with a married daughter. He reached the bedside just in time to grasp the old man's hand and, surrounded by the family congregated there, witness Daniel Muir's passing.

The younger Muir was likewise notified of his mother's impending death by supernatural means while at his writing desk in the second-floor study of his home in Martinez, California. The premonition arrived in late June 1896, but this time came with a greater sense of urgency. Already scheduled to leave within a few days to travel to Cambridge, Massachusetts, to receive an honorary degree from Harvard, he instead departed immediately for his mother's home in Portage, Wisconsin. Upon arriving, Muir discovered that she did, in fact, still live but that her heart was failing and that she was gravely ill, almost comatose. Anne Muir seemed to rally with the presence of her children—John had again convinced some of his siblings to act on his telepathic message—and, after a few days, the dutiful son boarded the train that would take him to Harvard. While en route, he received a wire in New York City saying that his mother had died in her sleep.

Relentless as a River of Ice

When Josiah Dwight Whitney was appointed the first California state geologist by legislative action on April 12, 1860, John Muir was still a year away from his first geology studies at the University of Wisconsin in Madison. Whitney graduated from Yale University with a degree in chemistry in 1839 while Muir was toddling about Dunbar, Scotland, in the year following his birth. Yet with the relentless, grinding force of glacial ice against granite, this pair played opposite one another in one of the most interesting scientific controversies of the late nineteenth century.

A leading and respected scientist of the day, Whitney was born in 1819 into a well-to-do family of thirteen children in Northampton, Massachusetts. Although educated in chemistry, he accepted a position with the New Hampshire Geological Survey and stayed on until the survey was completed in 1844. He then enrolled for advanced studies in chemistry and geology in Paris and at the University of Berlin. Upon returning to

America he went to work on a survey of Lake Superior, after which his education, training, and demonstrated value kept him in demand. He was engaged in geological surveys in New York, Michigan, Wisconsin, Illinois, and Iowa—these, in addition to a long and distinguished career as a professor and scientist at Harvard.

As state geologist, the California legislation made him responsible for "an accurate and complete Geological Survey of the State . . . with a full and scientific description of its rocks, fossils, soils, and minerals," along with other assignments and duties. Almost from the survey's inception, Whitney was at odds with the politicians who employed him. A determined and principled man, he brooked no interference in the business of the survey, refusing to divulge the location of mineral deposits to insiders or to subvert the scientific purposes of the work to make it a mere inventory of opportunities for mining speculators. Many politicians had other ideas. The result was a reduction in funds allocated for his office, until, by 1868, he was supporting at least some of the work of the survey at his own expense. Token appropriations were made in subsequent years but in 1874, the office of state geologist was politicized by placing it under authority of the governor and Whitney resigned in protest.

The geologist was not an innocent bystander through all this. He was, in fact, often fuel for the political fires that were consuming him. Obstinate and opinionated, he refused to compromise or negotiate, seldom even treated his sponsors in a civil manner, patronizing them rudely and condescendingly lecturing them. "Jackasses" was how he sometimes referred to the legislators who controlled the purse strings. Governor

Newton Booth said of him, "By no other man have I ever been so insulted in my life."

Despite political difficulties, the survey accomplished much. The members of the survey and mapping teams constantly rode, hiked, and climbed over remote and inhospitable terrain, from scorched deserts to icy mountain slopes, hefting heavy equipment and supplies much of the way. They spent months sleeping in tents and eating monotonous camp cooking, often in short supply. Still, by the end of 1862, the western half of California had been covered, with field workers logging some nine thousand linear miles in their travels, more than two thousand of them afoot. During 1863, the teams surveyed much of the Central Valley, the Mojave Desert, and parts of the Sierra Nevada, including Yosemite Valley.

Much of the time Whitney accompanied his teams in their travels, dividing his days between fieldwork and office duties. He was with them in June 1863 at Yosemite, and like most people who saw the place, Whitney and his workers were amazed at it. They speculated on the origins of the valley. Erosion was discussed. Ice-polished rocks and moraines brought glaciers into the conversations, but Whitney did not think such glory could result from such slow-acting processes and insisted that some cataclysm, or series of such events, was responsible. He believed that for unknown causes and by processes not understood the earth's crust beneath the place had suddenly subsided and the land that would become the valley floor crashed into the void, shearing off and carrying with it the mountainsides, creating the walls of the gorge. Contrary to scientific method, which requires questioning assumptions and changing one's mind when new knowledge requires it, this idea froze in Whitney's mind and refused to melt, no matter how much heat was generated by new and conflicting evidence. New and conflicting evidence was on the way, too, much of it courtesy of John Muir.

The story of Josiah Whitney, John Muir, and the glaciers of Yosemite, however, is not as simple as is often portrayed. For example, Whitney saw for himself that glaciers had been present in the valley, saw evidence of them, too, higher in the Sierra: "We are in the midst of what was once a great glacier region," he wrote of the view from Mount Dana, "the valleys all about being most superbly polished and grooved by glaciers, which once existed here on a stupendous scale." Nor was the notion of glaciers as the primary cause of the physical features of Yosemite Valley unheard of. That idea was presented to him in 1864—while Muir was in Canada and still four years away from Yosemite—by Clarence King, a member of his own survey party.

King, who would later become one of America's finest geologists and in 1879 would be named the first director of the United States Geological Survey, would also become a well-known mountaineer and writer. In 1863, though, he was just a young man with a degree in geology from Yale, and in search of adventure. He went to work for the California survey in September 1863, and late the next summer had earned enough trust to lead a special expedition to Yosemite Valley and the Mariposa Grove of sequoias. President Abraham Lincoln had set those areas aside "for public use, resort, and recreation" under management of the State of California, and King and his crew set out to map the boundaries. His notes from the survey detail his conclusions about glaciers, including seeing evidence of five tributary glaciers in the upper regions feeding one large one in the valley: "From a rough guess . . . nearly, if not a little over, a thousand feet thick." He felt "no shadow of a doubt" of glacial action.

Whitney disagreed. Although he had seen some of the evidence himself in 1863, and King's detailed report amplified the evidence, the state geologist refused to believe that glaciers had played a noteworthy role in creating the valley's magnificent landscape. In response, King changed his mind to conform with his superior. He wrote, in 1872, that while his thousand-foot glacier had existed, it had an insignificant effect in shoveling out the gorge. The last word on the subject, so far as Whitney was concerned, was written in his 1868 publication, *The Yosemite Book*. "A more absurd theory was never advanced, than that by which it is sought to ascribe to glaciers the sawing out of these vertical walls and the rounding of the domes," he wrote. "This theory, based on entire ignorance of the whole subject, may be dropped without wasting any more time on it."

Muir disagreed. While Whitney's opinions were the result of a professional geologist's many years of training, education, expertise, and experience, the amateur arrived at his conclusions using somewhat different methods. "No scientific book in the world can tell me how this Yosemite granite is put together or how it has been taken down," he wrote in an 1871 letter to Jeanne Carr. "Patient observation and constant brooding above the rocks, lying upon them for years as the ice did, is the way to arrive at the truths which are graven so lavishly upon them."

His 1871 journals, as well his letters—written while he lived in the valley, running a sawmill and doing odd jobs for the hotel keeper James Hutchings—tell, often in ecstatic language, how he arrived at these truths. He wrote in his journal of standing atop Sentinel Dome overlooking Yosemite Valley, and described the scene as it must have looked in ages past, with "no rock to interrupt the snowy expanse, which waves gently, heaving and rising in one huge general sheet." He talked of summer, when "the surface of the icy sea resounds with the song of running waters." Time passes, and, "later, as the long icy centuries circle away, the first of the valley rocks is seen bare and bright on the north wall." Then, he wrote, later still, "Winters and summers come and go with their storm clouds and balmy sun-days, like those of the present time, and the main Yosemite glacier shrinks slowly until its wasting snout reaches no farther than the base of El Capitan." In a September 8 letter he said, "The grandeur of these forces and their glorious results overpower me and inhabit my whole being. Waking or sleeping, I have no rest. In dreams I read blurred sheets of glacial writing."

Of course, there was more to his studies of glaciers than brooding, imagining, and dreaming. "When I came to moraines, or ice scratches upon the rocks, I traced them, learning what I could of the glacier that made them," he wrote. "I asked the boulders I met whence they came and whither they were going . . . and when I discovered a mountain or rock of marked form or structure, I climbed about it." Like King, he discerned evidence of five tributary glaciers carving their channels to the bottom of the main canyon. He found smaller tributaries as well, terminating high above. The evidence seemed clear: "So fully are the works of these vanished glaciers recorded upon the clean, unblurred pages of the mountains that it is difficult to assure ourselves that centuries have elapsed since they vanished."

Nor was he uninformed concerning the textbook principles behind glaciation and the state of science on the subject. While under the tutelage of Professor Ezra Carr at the University of Wisconsin, Muir studied geology and was especially taken with the theories of Harvard scientist Louis Agassiz. Since coming to the United States from Europe in 1848, Agassiz had turned loose on the American landscape his knowledge of how glaciers behaved in the Swiss Alps. His ideas on glacial motion and its results spurred widespread study and interest among many, including Muir. In fact, as Muir's evidence mounted, he would relay it to Agassiz by mail and learn in reply that the professor considered him the first man to have truly grasped the concept of glacial action. The two narrowly missed meeting in 1872, when the Harvard scientist planned a trip to Yosemite but was taken ill while visiting San Francisco and unable to make the journey.

Other scientists, however, had made the trip, and Muir never missed an opportunity to preach to them his gospel on glaciers. First came Joseph LeConte, geology professor at the University of California and acquaintance of Jeanne Carr, who told him of Muir's studies and supplied a letter of introduction. Traveling with a student group in the summer of 1870, the professor invited the then sawmill operator to guide them around the valley and accompany them up the Sierra. For days, Muir pointed out evidence of glaciers and expounded on their accomplishments. LeConte left convinced, for the most part, of the accuracy of Muir's ideas and from then on passed them along in lectures.

A September 8, 1871, letter from Muir to Jeanne Carr told of another visit from the ivory towers. "Professor [John Daniel] Runkle, president of the Boston Institute of Technology, was here last week," he wrote. After several days in the canyon and high country, "He was fully convinced of the truth of my readings and urged me to write out the glacial system of Yosemite and its tributaries for the Boston Academy of Science." Muir agreed to send along his thoughts, with permission to publish the paper if "his wise scientific brothers thought it of sufficient interest."

He did piece together an article, cannibalized from letters to friends, but sent it instead to the *New York Daily Tribune* where it was published under the headline YOSEMITE GLACIERS on December 5, 1871. It was the reluctant author's first published work and he earned two hundred dollars for the effort, in addition to exposure in one of the country's most influential newspapers. In it, he wrote, "glaciers work apart from men, exerting their tremendous energies in silence and darkness . . . working unwearied through unmeasured times, unhalting as the stars, until at length, their creations complete . . . calm as when they came as crystals from the sky, they depart." That publication was followed, in December 1872, with "The Living Glaciers of California" in the San Francisco literary magazine *The Overland Monthly*. Later, he developed a seven-part series, "Studies in the Sierra," for that periodical, which appeared in 1874 and 1875 issues, complete with maps and diagrams detailing the glacial process, as well as divulging the locations of glaciers still in existence and at work.

Muir's theory of glacial creation of the Yosemite Valley and its effects throughout the Sierra were now a matter of public record. The ideas of the amateur geologist, however, were a direct refutation of the professional, Josiah Whitney. The professor's views were widely distributed in two books drawn from the work of the California Geological Survey, *The Yosemite Book,* published in 1868, an oversized and expensive volume illustrated with photographs, and the *Yosemite Guide-Book,* which followed. Popular for more than a decade, the smaller volume was reprinted several times and sold widely throughout California and to the tourist trade. Muir was often questioned by Whitney's readers, and he never hesitated to correct the professor's theories, often with strong words—but no stronger than the expert geologist's claim in *The Yosemite Book* that "A more absurd theory was never advanced" than that claiming glaciers formed the valley. However, that statement did not reflect directly on his nemesis, as Muir had only just arrived in California the year the book was published. But later, the Harvard professor resented being challenged by "that sheep herder," whom he also called an "ignoramus," and said finally in 1882 that "there are no glaciers at all in the Sierra."

Clarence King, in his 1878 book, *Systematic Geology,* defended his former employer at Muir's expense, particularly against the claim that active glaciers were still at their work in the Sierra. "It is to be hoped that Mr. Muir's vagaries will not deceive geologists who are personally unacquainted with California," he wrote, "and that the ambitious amateur himself may divert his evident enthusiastic love of nature into a channel, if there is one, in which his attainments would save him from hopeless floundering."

Whitney died in August 1896. Apparently Muir had not

borne a grudge, for when he and others organized the Sierra Club in 1892, the eminent professor Whitney was enrolled as an honorary member. While there may have developed a grudging respect between Muir and King, the geologist's attacks on the mountaineer were never forgotten, nor were the cutting remarks Muir, in turn, made about the geologist's skill—or lack of it—as a mountaineer. King died on December 24, 1901, at age fifty-nine.

Since, whether practiced by amateurs or professionals, the job of science is to reveal truth, science eventually proved Muir's theory correct in all its essentials. His main departure from the facts resulted from following the belief of Agassiz that most of the work of glaciers was accomplished in a single great ice age, when, in fact, giant ice sheets had advanced and retreated on several occasions. The argument seems to have been settled beyond question by 1930 when a United States Geological Survey publication said, "In neither the Yosemite nor in any other valley of its type is there evidence of any dislocation of the earth's crust," and, "Muir was probably as nearly right in his glacial theory of the Yosemite as any scientist in the early [eighteen-] seventies could have been."

Traveling Planet Earth

A humanities professor at the University of Wisconsin passed along to his students Ralph Waldo Emerson's advice that they keep a "commonplace book," a journal recording ideas and observations, opinions and interpretations. At least one scholar followed the recommendation. In a fresh notebook in which he would chronicle an extended trip, he inscribed his name and address: "John Muir, Earth-planet, Universe." He made that notation in September 1867, as he set out on his thousand-mile walk through the Southern states to the Gulf of Mexico. At age twenty-eight, he was already fairly well traveled, given his time and circumstances.

Until age eleven, Muir's travels had been limited to boyhood romps through the hills and along the rocky coast of the North Sea near his hometown of Dunbar, Scotland. Then one day, his father told the boy he needn't finish his school studies that evening as they were leaving for America come the morning. So began a journey he would never complete—a life of wandering the "Earth-planet," sometimes with a destination in mind but just as often for the sheer joy of seeing new places and unfamiliar things.

Of his initial journey, he recalled, "we went by rail to Glasgow and thence joyfully sailed away from beloved Scotland, flying to our fortunes on the wings of the winds, care-free as thistle seeds." The year was 1849, and the young traveler said that "In crossing the Atlantic before the days of steamships, or even the American clippers, the voyages made in old fashioned sailing-vessels were very long. Ours was six weeks and three days." But the time was not wasted for Muir and his younger brother, he said. "That long voyage had not a dull moment for us boys."

Father Daniel Muir had left Scotland for the New World without a specific destination in mind. He gave some thought to Canada, but abandoned the idea based on shipboard discussions. While he and other passengers weighed the alternatives, the young boys were otherwise occupied. "As we neared the shore of the great new land, with what eager wonder we watched the whales and dolphins and porpoises and seabirds," Muir said, "and made the good-natured sailors teach us their names and tell us stories about them!"

Daniel Muir learned from a New York grain merchant, his own trade in Scotland, that he saw fine shipments of grain coming in from Wisconsin. Upon learning that others of his religious persuasion were settling there, he and the boys made their way to the Wisconsin wilderness to carve out a frontier farm. Young John found the arrival as joyful as the departure. "This sudden plash into pure wildness—baptism in Nature's warm heart—how utterly happy it made us!" he wrote.

Hard work soon dimmed his fervor and kept his feet firmly planted in the soil of the family farms until 1860 when he left for Madison and the Wisconsin State Agricultural Society Fair. The success of the inventions he exhibited led to a winter job across the state at Prairie du Chien on the shores of the Mississippi River, but he found the work unsatisfying and journeyed back to Madison to enroll at the University of Wisconsin. At the end of the spring term in 1863, tired and hungry from the spartan life he was forced to live as a student, he set out to seek relief in the wild. "From the top of a hill on the north side of Lake Mendota I gained a last wistful, lingering view of the University grounds and buildings," he wrote. "There with streaming eyes I bade my blessed Alma Mater farewell. But I was only leaving one University for another, the Wisconsin University for the University of the Wilderness."

His course of study at his new school included geology and botany; his text the Wisconsin River valley. He followed the stream westward across the southern part of the state to its union with the Mississippi, then crossed the big river into Iowa. Along the way he collected flowers and plants, cataloged ferns and mosses, studied rock formations and outcroppings along the bluffs, and hiked and climbed and explored as days turned into weeks.

Ready again to face the more conventional demands of the world by July 1863, he returned to his family's Fountain Lake Farm, most of which had been cleared and built with his own hands but was now owned by a brother-in-law, to handle chores and help with the harvest. He helped another brother-in-law build a house and worked for a brother cutting firewood, all the while parrying family queries about the course of his future. The threat of the military draft for Civil War service loomed; a threat he grew increasingly unwilling to face. He considered attending medical school, but opted to work through the winter, save money, and perhaps return to Scotland. It was a journey he would not make. Instead, on March 1, 1864, he boarded a northbound train in Portage, Wisconsin, and took a trip into Canada that would occupy his next two years.

Sketchy information suggests he left his home state at its northern border and entered Michigan's Upper Peninsula, then crossed into Canada at Sault Sainte Marie, putting him above Lake Huron's western extreme. From there he slogged eastward through wetlands and woods along the shores of the lake's North Channel, veering southeast along the edge of Georgian Bay to its southern tip, a distance of at least two hundred and fifty miles. On the way he collected plants in the bitterly cold boreal bogs. The highlight of his botany season was the discovery of a rare orchid, *Calypso borealis,* the "hider of the north," a find that renewed his spirits after a particularly dismal day splashing through a frigid swamp. Overcome by its beauty, he sat beside the flower and wept.

He continued hiking southward beyond the bay, and in June made the town of Bradford, Ontario, where he laid over for a time with a family of Scottish immigrants, then continued south to Lake Ontario's Burlington Bay and east to Niagara Falls. There, he linked up with his younger brother, Daniel, who was also using the border as protection against the military drafts back home. By then, Muir's Canadian trek had covered nearly four hundred miles, almost every one of them over difficult and seldom-traveled terrain.

The Muir brothers returned to the southern tip of Georgian

Bay, taking up work for the winter in a lumber mill and wooden-tool manufactory near the Ontario town of Meaford. Daniel returned to Wisconsin in the spring; John stayed on to work at the mill and wander the woods. His strolling through the forests studying plants must have seemed odd to settlers in the area, for, in a September 13, 1865 letter to Jeanne Carr, Muir wrote, "In my long rambles last summer I did not find a single person who knew anything of botany and but a few who knew the meaning of the word." Fire ended the sawmill and woodworking job prematurely, and he left Ontario and returned to the United States almost two years to the day after setting out on his Canadian sojourn.

The twenty-eight-year-old Muir worked at a wagon parts factory in Indianapolis, Indiana, for almost a year until temporarily blinded by an on-the-job-accident. Determined to abandon the settled life, he set out on his thousand-mile walk from Louisville, Kentucky to Florida's Gulf Coast.

He recorded the journey in the notebook in which he declared himself a resident of "Earth-planet, Universe." The account begins with Muir's explanation for choosing his route. "I had long been looking from the wild woods and gardens of the Northern States to those of the warm South," he wrote, "and at last, all drawbacks overcome, I set forth on the first day of September, 1867, joyful and free, on a thousand-mile walk to the Gulf of Mexico."

Although already well-aware that few of his fellow humans shared his fascination with nature, that realization was reinforced before his journey was a week old. Muir reported that when he asked a Kentuckian about a nearby natural wonder, "He told me that he had never been at Mammoth Cave—that it was not worth going ten miles to see, as it was nothing but a hole in the ground, and I found that his was no rare case." The native, he wrote, "was one of the useful, practical men—too wise to waste precious time with weeds, caves, fossils, or anything else he could not eat."

The journey had its adventuresome moments. He faced cold, hunger, and fatigue, spending most nights outdoors. Corn bread, bacon, and crackers were the staples of his diet, and he had little of that most days and none at all others. Food was difficult to obtain owing to the poverty he encountered along his backwoods route. Some people would not share or sell any of their meager stores out of fear and suspicion of the ragged traveler.

He faced down bandits and highwaymen. A lone horseman once offered to carry his satchel, but left Muir in the dust once he had the bag in hand. The robber galloped ahead and stopped to rifle through the bag, then returned it in disgust when he found nothing of value. On another occasion, near sundown, a band of ten horseback ruffians riding abreast along the road ahead stopped to watch the explorer approach. Muir wrote, "there was nothing for it but to face them fearlessly, without showing the slightest suspicion of foul play." As he neared, he smiled and gave the men a "howdy" then walked around them. One hundred and fifty yards down the road, without breaking stride, he glanced back and saw that the men had turned their horses in his direction and were, he believed, discussing whether or not to rob him. "I was not followed, however," he wrote, "probably because the plants projecting from my plant press made them believe I was a poor herb doctor."

Along with adventure, his journal chronicled personal discoveries such as his first encounter with Tennessee's Emory River. "There is nothing more eloquent in Nature than a mountain stream, and this is the first I ever saw," he said. On its flower-covered banks under a canopy of trees, he wrote that he "Lingered in this sanctuary a long time thanking the Lord with all my heart for his goodness in allowing me to enter and enjoy it." Nearly a month afoot in the mountains and woods did not temper his enthusiasm. A September 29 note includes his keenness for a heretofore unknown plant: "To-day I met a magnificent grass, ten or twelve feet in stature, with a superb panicle of glossy purple flowers. Its leaves, too, are of princely mould and dimensions."

Ten days later he found himself surrounded by civilization and in a different frame of mind. "Reached Savannah, but find no word from home," he wrote, "and the money that I had ordered to be sent by express from Portage by my brother had not yet arrived. Feel dreadfully lonesome and poor." He used the little money he had to buy crackers and camped out among the tombs in a graveyard. It was, he said, "an ideal place for a penniless wanderer. There no superstitious prowling mischief maker dares venture for fear of haunting ghosts, while for me there will be God's rest and peace."

Immediately upon receiving the expected funds he left town and boarded a ship for a trip down the inland waterway along the Georgia coast, bypassing practically impassable swamps blocking the way south, only to find similar obstacles awaiting at the end of the voyage. "Florida is so watery and vine-tied that pathless wanderings are not easily possible in any direction," he wrote. "I started to cross the State by a gap hewn for the locomotive, walking sometimes between the rails, stepping from tie to tie, or walking on the strip of sand at the sides, gazing into the mysterious forest, Nature's own." Still, he remained fervent: "It is almost impossible to write the dimmest picture of plant grandeur so redundant, unfathomable," and a few days later, "Swamp very dense during this day's journey. Almost one continuous sheet of water covered with aquatic trees and vines." He added, "No stream that I crossed to-day appeared to have the least idea where it was going."

Although he had been aboard ship on the Atlantic just over a week earlier, reaching the shores of the Gulf of Mexico near Cedar Keys triggered old memories. "To-day I reached the sea," his journal entry for October 23, 1867, reads. "While I was yet many miles back in the palmy woods, I caught the scent of the salt sea breeze which, although I had so many years lived far from the sea breezes, suddenly conjured up Dunbar, its rocky coast, winds and waves."

He intended to linger among the sea breezes of the Gulf coast only long enough to catch a ride on a southbound ship and fulfill the dream of visiting South America as Alexander von Humboldt had done. He learned that a ship was due within a few weeks to take on lumber bound for the Texas coast. With luck, he could hitch a ride to Galveston and from there to the West Indies and find passage on yet another southbound vessel. He hired on at a sawmill to pass the time and earn some money, but the ship came and went without Muir for he was stricken with malaria and barely alive when it set sail.

Lethargy and headaches weakened him, he said, then "the fever broke on me like a storm, and before I had staggered halfway to the mill I fell down unconscious on the narrow trail." He lay there into the night, awoke and again tried to reach the mill but after staggering only a hundred yards collapsed. A later attempt brought him to the stairway leading to the mill, where he fell unconscious again. The night watchman ignored him, thinking him a passed-out drunk. Fortunately, the mill owner diagnosed malaria and dosed Muir with quinine. Typhoid and dropsy also affected him, and he was forced to lounge around Cedar Keys, with little strength to do anything but sit on the beach and study the local flora and fauna. "During my long sojourn here as a convalescent," he wrote, "I used to lie on my back for whole days beneath the ample arms of these great trees [live oaks], listening to the winds and the birds."

The lassitude and illness clung to him until early January 1868. He finally boarded a ship, this one bound for Cuba, hoping to continue south from there. Instead, he found himself marooned in the harbor at Havana, lacking means or opportunity to leave. He developed a taste for tropical fruits, including his first taste of pineapple. The sailors willingly rowed him ashore to Havana as often as he wanted, but he wanted more: "How, I wondered, shall I be able to escape from this great city confusion? How shall I reach nature in this delectable land?" He eventually found some solace in nearby forests and on quiet beaches, but his body, weak from malaria and suffering occasional relapses, allowed little of the vigorous exploring he craved. Still, he was loath to abandon the journey. "I made up my mind to push on to South America while my stock of strength, such as it was, lasted. . . . I had long wished to visit the Orinoco basin and in particular the basin of the Amazon."

Again, he was disappointed and forced to adjust his plans.

"After visiting all the shipping agencies, I could not find a vessel of any sort bound for South America, and so made up a plan to go North, to the longed-for cold weather of New York, and thence to the forests and mountains of California," he wrote. "There, I thought, I shall find health and new plants and mountains, and after a year spent in that interesting country I can carry out my Amazon plans."

His 1868 arrival in California was the result of disappoint ment and happenstance, but the state would become the base of operations for the wanderer's travels for the remainder of his life. From there, too, he would carry out his Amazon plans, although forty-three years later. For the next nine years, in fact, he would not cross his adopted state's borders. During that time, he walked and rode horse- and muleback far and wide up and down both sides of the state's Sierra, climbing most of the peaks in the range—first to reach the top of many—exploring the valleys, becoming intimately familiar with the plants and animals, and coming to know more of the geological history of the area than any contemporary.

Muir worked from time to time at a variety of jobs—horse breaker, ranch hand, sheepherder, sawmill operator, hotel caretaker, tourist guide, writer—but he worked solely to support his wanderings and the study and contemplation they afforded. He seldom lived far from Yosemite, and often within the confines of the valley.

Not until 1877 would he venture outside California, then traveling to Utah Territory to explore the Wasatch Mountains. Though six hundred miles apart, the Wasatch and Sierra ranges are geologically linked as opposite rims of the Great Basin, a huge inland drainage containing the western half of

Utah, most of Nevada, and bits of Idaho, Wyoming, Oregon, and California.

During his Utah visit, Muir watched one of the "grandest storms" he had ever seen. "Wind, rain, and snow filled the whole basin [meaning the Salt Lake Valley between the Wasatch and Oquirrh mountains], driving wildly over valley and plain from range to range," he wrote on May 17. "Toward the evening of the 18th it began to wither. The snowy skirts of the Wasatch Mountains appeared beneath the lifting fringes of the clouds, and the sun shone out through colored windows, producing one of the most glorious after-storm effects I ever witnessed." The Oquirrhs, he said, were gilded beyond recognition with ethereal gold, the plain painted red and purple. "I felt," he wrote, "as if newly arrived in some other far-off world."

From Utah, Muir returned briefly to Yosemite, then explored the San Gabriel Mountains and Valley northeast of Los Angeles. His next journey took him north, when, in September, he accompanied Harvard professor and botanist Asa Gray on an expedition to Mount Shasta and the region where the headwaters of the Sacramento River rose.

The two had met in 1872, an acquaintance arranged by Jeanne Carr, who told the eminent scientist of her friend's interest in botany. Gray arrived on Muir's doorstep one July day asking to see interesting and unusual plants. For a week, the amateur led the most famous botanist in America around the valley and atop the cliffs above. Impressed with his guide's knowledge, Gray urged him to come to Harvard and take up the academic life. Muir declined but the two maintained contact and over the years many of Muir's plant specimens were added to Gray's collections at Harvard.

On the way to Mount Shasta, Gray's party stopped off at Rancho Chico, home of John Bidwell. Their host had been a member of the first organized immigrant party to California in 1841. He struck it rich as a miner during the California gold rush and used his fortune to establish the twenty-six-thousand-acre ranching empire at Chico. The well-liked and respected "Prince of Pioneers" had served as a state senator and California's representative to Congress, attained the rank of major in the Mexican War, and brigadier general in the California militia.

This accidental meeting of Muir and Bidwell proved rewarding. In one another they found common interests, both being accomplished, if amateur, botanists and geologists. The friendship that resulted from the chance acquaintance lasted thirty-seven years. When Gray returned east several days later, Muir stayed with the Bidwells for two extra weeks, time the new friends spent studying plants and examining rock formations in the mountains of northern California.

When he decided to return home, the traveler enlisted the aid of his host's carpenters to hammer together a crude little boat he could captain downriver. First christened the *Spoonbill*, the leaky craft was soon renamed *Snagjumper* in honor of its ability to ride over obstacles in the stream. From Bidwell's landing on the Sacramento River, Muir floated and sailed downstream for five days, reaching the confluence with the American River at Sacramento on October 8, 1877.

River running must have seemed agreeable to Muir, for a month later he built another small boat at Hopeton in the Sierra foothills below Yosemite, christened it *Snagjumper II*, and rowed and drifted down the Merced and San Joaquin Rivers to the town of Martinez, a two-hundred-fifty-mile float. Once ashore, he walked a few miles to visit for the first time the home of horticulturist Dr. John Strentzel, who would become his father-in-law, and Louie Wanda Strentzel, who became his wife.

The following summer, 1878, took the traveler again to the Great Basin, this time with the United States Coast and Geodetic Survey to trace the thirty-ninth parallel across Nevada's basin and range country. While away, he wrote several letters to the Strentzel family, accelerating the pace of his courtship of Louie. He noted in his letters visiting a number of abandoned mining camps and works in Nevada, some of which had turned from thriving towns to ghosts in only a decade. He told of the infamous Forty-Mile Desert, a waterless stretch on the California Trail between the sinks of the Humboldt and Carson Rivers. His most dramatic letter, dated August 28, told of a near-fatal adventure at Lone Mountain, near the town of Belmont in south-central Nevada.

In the letter, he first exclaimed on the beauty of nature, calling the "falling water, cloud drapery, thunder tones, lightning, and blue sky windows" of summer thundershowers marching across the desert "one of the most impressive pictures I have ever beheld." He then related his exciting discovery of evidence of glacial activity, which was so obscured in the eroded mountains that "only the skilled observer could detect" it.

Then, "against my counsel and remonstrances while forty miles from any known water," Muir wrote, he and the two other men in the party ascended Lone Mountain. "Two of the three nearly lost their lives," he said. The two collapsed after making it down the mountain, leaving Muir to locate the horses and pack animals, rescue his comrades, and take them to water. "We reached water at daybreak of the second day—two days and nights in this fire without water!"

The next major journey would take the explorer to a moister, if no less perilous place. It would also be his last jaunt as a bachelor, he and Louie having agreed to marry upon his return—whenever that might be. On July 10, 1879, he boarded a mail steamer out of Portland, Oregon, bound for Alaska to study the glaciers there. The first notable event of the journey was the attempted ascent of Glenora Peak, during which he saved his climbing partner, the missionary S. Hall Young, from an almost certain death by rescuing him from a near fall over a thousand-foot precipice, then carrying him down the mountain. Later, Muir and Young, guided by Alaskan natives, paddled canoes through the maze of islands and inlets along Alaska's southern coast to discover Glacier Bay. He left Alaska in late December and arrived at the Strentzel Ranch in California after speaking engagements in Portland and San Francisco. By the end of July 1880, he was again on the way to Alaska, this time taking with him the blessing of Louie, now Mrs. John Muir.

This trip was a brief one, undertaken to explore fjords and arms of Glacier Bay that bad weather and the lateness of the season had prevented visiting the year before. He and missionary Young set out from Fort Wrangell for Glacier Bay, reached the place in five days, and spent the weeks to come exploring and mapping.

Accompanying the expedition was the missionary's Alaskan mutt, Stickeen, whose adventures while stranded with Muir on a glacier would become one of the naturalist's most popular stories.

Muir returned to California where, by fall, he was hard at work in the fields and orchards given him and Louie as a wedding gift by the Strentzels. The work would limit—practically eliminate—his travels for most of the decade to come. His feet never stopped itching, however. He would finally journey to South America, the original object of his wanderlust, and, eventually, circumnavigate "Earth-planet, Universe." But all that would come later.

The Sage and the Sierra

J ohn Muir was intimately familiar with some of the world's most inspiring landscapes and acquainted with many famous and influential figures. He witnessed earth-changing events, both natural and man-made; his accomplishments and adventures filled books. Among a long list of memorable incidents in his life are two he considered the most remarkable: his discovery of a rare orchid, *Calypso borealis*, in a Canadian swamp, and meeting Ralph Waldo Emerson, "the Sage of Concord," the premier literary figure of the day.

Born in Boston in 1803, Emerson came from a long line of churchmen, and was himself an ordained Unitarian minister who left the pulpit owing to doctrinal doubts. The Harvard graduate published his first book in 1836. It attracted little notice at the time, but the volume contained the essence of the philosophy of Transcendentalism, which celebrated introspection and individualism, and advocated that a higher reality was possible than that reached through the senses or reason. His literary credits over the years included several volumes of essays and poetry. His essays were widely read and his poetry included the "Concord Hymn," a tribute to the Revolutionary War.

Muir learned of Emerson during his college days at the University of Wisconsin in Madison, both in his course work and through the influence of his friend and mentor, Jeanne Carr, who numbered the poet and philosopher among her personal friends. The student found the New Englander's writings congenial and read and reread his works. Those books were still among Muir's valued possessions when he was running a sawmill and working as hotel handyman in the Yosemite Valley in May 1871, when a letter from Carr arrived. "I am feeling as glad for you as possible since Mr. Emerson will be in the Valley in a few days—and in your hands I hope and trust," she said. She also wrote that she would "send Mr. Emerson a note . . . about you."

Ten of Emerson's friends and family members left San Francisco with the essayist, who, at age sixty-eight, still enjoyed widespread popularity and influence but suffered from failing health and was no longer writing. Luggage for the rugged journey was limited, but Emerson insisted on bringing along his prized purple satchel, loaded with a few favorite books for study and enjoyment and the letter of introduction to Muir, provided by Jeanne Carr. The party arrived at Yosemite on May 8, the day Muir received his letter from Carr announcing the philosopher's visit, and spent their first two days there touring on horseback. "This valley," the well-traveled Emerson said, "is the only place that comes up to the brag about it, and exceeds it."

No one noticed a shy sawyer hanging about the fringes of the admiring crowds that surrounded the famous visitor at the hotel in the evening. Muir dared not approach the celebrated poet, despite his eagerness and the expectation, based on Carr's letter, that he would be known to Emerson. Instead, he wrote a note of his own and had it delivered to the hotel. In it, he expressed regret at hearing that the party would be leaving in just a few days. "Now Mr. Emerson I do most cordially protest against your going away so soon, and so also I am sure do all your instincts and yearnings." Then he made a bold counteroffer.

"I invite you to join me in a months [sic] worship with Nature in the high temples of the great Sierra crown beyond our holy Yosemite," he wrote. "It will cost you nothing save the time and very little of that for you will be mostly in eternity." The letter continued with more praise for the high country, then, "in the name of all the spirit creatures of these rocks and of this whole spiritual atmosphere," it concluded with, "Do not leave us now. With most cordial regards I am yours in Nature, John Muir."

The next morning, an eager Emerson arrived at the sawmill where Muir worked and where he also lived in a "nest" he had built under the overhang of the building's eaves, accessible only by climbing a "chicken ladder" of planks and cleats. The frail philosopher gamely made the climb and the two pored over Muir's drawings and diagrams, rock and plant specimens. The visitor must have felt welcome and enjoyed the visit, for according to his host, "He came again and again, and I saw him every day while he remained in the Valley."

On all of those days, the explorer regaled his guest with tales of his Sierra expeditions, of weeks spent in high country solitude, and lobbied the man he admired to leave his cautious entourage behind and go with him into the wilderness. Family and friends prevailed, however, and would not allow it. On May 11, Emerson enjoyed apple pie for breakfast—after all, he asked a tablemate, "What is pie for?"—and was horseback and on the trail to the Mariposa Grove of giant sequoias shortly afterward. Muir agreed to accompany him, but only "if you promise to camp with me in the Grove," to which his friend agreed.

As the group rode horseback down the trail, the Eastern literati in the party talked books and writers with the rough-hewn explorer, and one of them, only barely impressed, labeled him a "botanist mainly" but also "an interesting young fellow, of real intelligence and character." The group reached a roadhouse and began preparations to spend the night. When he asked about the plan to camp out under the big trees, Muir was told by Emerson's people that they could not risk it, as the old philosopher might catch cold. He could not dissuade them, despite his claim that there wasn't "a single cough or sneeze in all the Sierra." In the end, he too decided to stay at the inn so he could remain close to Emerson, and was happy to spend the time "warming in the light of his face as at a fire."

They visited the sequoia grove the next day, under the guidance of the innkeeper, who had vast knowledge of the trees. The tourists were astounded at the size of the ancient evergreens. Fallen trunks were higher than the head of a man on horseback, and one rider actually rode inside a downed tree that had been hollowed by fire. The largest tree in the grove, a living sequoia called the Grizzly Giant, could not be encircled by thirteen mounted riders—they determined six more would be required to finish the job. A single limb on the Giant, more than six and a half feet in diameter, was bigger around, they realized, than the *trunk* of any tree in the Eastern forests they loved. The guide invited Emerson to select and name a big tree and "Samoset" was chosen to honor a Pemaquid Indian leader who had aided the Pilgrims in colonial Massachusetts.

They enjoyed lunch in the grove, and again Muir complained that the vacationers were leaving the Sierra without staying long enough or seeing enough to fully appreciate the wonder and beauty of his mountain home. "It is as if a photographer should remove his plate before the impression was fully made," he said. The party was determined, however, and after eating remounted for the ride back to the roadhouse where they would board stagecoaches bound for San Francisco. He did not accompany them, deciding to camp alone among the sequoia if the Sage of Concord would not camp with him. As the group topped a ridge whose other side would take them out of Muir's sight, Emerson lagged behind and stopped his horse on the skyline, turned his mount back toward where his newfound friend stood below, and, with his hat, waved a long good-bye. The saddened mountaineer, "though lonesome for the first time in those forests," soon rallied, realizing that "the trees had not gone to Boston, nor the birds; and as I sat by the fire, Emerson was still with me in spirit."

Muir and the Transcendentalist wrote many letters to one another thereafter, those eastbound often containing pressed flowers and sprigs of fragrant incense cedar to conjure memories of the Sierra and Yosemite. The philosopher repeatedly encouraged the mountaineer to come east to New England to visit him and others of similar spirit, including botanist Asa Gray and Harvard scientist Louis Agassiz.

Emerson died in 1882 and was buried in Concord. Among his personal papers was a list headed "My Men." Fewer than twenty names were on the list, men with whom the poet and philosopher felt a particular kinship, or believed to be exceptionally influential, intelligent, or important. Henry David Thoreau was there. So was Agassiz. Also listed were the writer and professor Oliver Wendell Holmes, and British historian Thomas Carlyle. At the bottom of the list, as his final entry, he had penciled in "John Muir."

In an undated journal entry Muir said, "Emerson was the most serene, majestic, sequoia-like soul I ever met. . . . I sensed here was the man I had been seeking." On a trip to the East in 1893 he made certain to stop by Emerson's grave in Sleepy Hollow Cemetery.

Nature at Its Worst

No one needs to dig deep into John Muir's life to uncover his love for nature's beauty. Nor does he bury his appreciation for the wilder side of nature—his account of an 1874 tree ride in a furious Sierra gale, for example, is a favorite tale. Less well-known is that the explorer and naturalist found glory in the natural world at its most violent, destructive, and dangerous. He found crushing icebergs, shifting glaciers, avalanches, even earthquakes awe-inspiring and worthy of praise. He seldom let weather extremes, whether heat or cold or wind or storm, affect his activities. Even grizzly bears, rattlesnakes, coyotes, and other creatures most humans either anxiously avoid or eagerly destroy, were objects of his admiration.

In writing about the grizzlies that once inhabited California's Sierra Nevada, he said the animal, although seldom seen, was then widespread in an "Eden" of ever-present and easily obtainable food. He appreciated their ability to eat anything, claiming that practically every part of every plant fed the bruin, as would rodents, squirrels, lizards, ants, wasps, and a host of other creatures. "What digestion!" he wrote. "A sheep or a wounded deer or a pig he eats warm, about as quickly as a boy eats a buttered muffin; or should the meat be a month old, it is still welcomed with tremendous relish."

Muir himself once feared becoming a meal for a Sierra bear. The encounter—"interview" he called it—happened during his first visit to the mountains north of Yosemite Valley in 1869. He discovered the grizzly in a small meadow and watched it for some time from the concealment of the woods. Deciding he would like to see how the bear looked while running, to "study his gait," the mountaineer rushed out of the forest toward it, hoping to frighten it away. "But, contrary to all I had heard about the shyness of bears, he did not run at all," Muir wrote, "and when I stopped short within a few steps of him, as he held his ground in a fighting attitude, my mistake was monstrously plain." While he managed to back away from the interview un-eaten, even unhurt, the effect was lasting: "I was then put on my good behavior, and never afterward forgot the right manners of the wilderness."

In an essay about Yosemite National Park in his 1901 book *Our National Parks,* Muir confessed, "Before I learned to re-spect rattlesnakes I killed two. . . . At that time, thirty years ago, I imagined that rattlesnakes should be killed whenever found." While crossing central California's San Joaquin plain, he surprised a rattler stretched across the trail and stomped it to death. The other was killed a few years later in a cabin where Muir was living in Yosemite Valley. He discovered the snake hiding in a corner beneath a pile of plants collected for study, and although the rattler seemed embarrassed at being caught where it did not belong, "as if wishing the ground would open and hide him," the cabin's rightful occupant decided the snake must be sacrificed for the safety of the many people, including children, who visited there. "Since then," he said, "I have seen perhaps a hundred or more in these mountains, but I have never intentionally disturbed them."

He did, however, disturb one in precarious circumstances while climbing out of Tuolumne Canyon in Yosemite National Park. Scrambling up a slope of earthquake talus, his passage was blocked by a boulder so large that even stretched to the limits of his height he could barely reach the top. The rattlesnake was apparently sunning itself atop the hunk of granite and as Muir pulled himself up he saw the coiled snake as soon as his eyes cleared the top edge of the rock. He wrote: "My hands had alarmed him, and he was ready for me; but even with this provocation, and when my head came in sight within a foot of him, he did not strike."

Muir did not say how he escaped the encounter. He did, however, praise snakes in the essay, calling them "mostly handsome and harmless" and claimed that none of the thousands of tourists who had visited the park had ever been bitten. He said that some of the snakes "vie with the lizards in beauty of color and dress patterns. Only the rattlesnake is venomous, and he carefully keeps to himself as far as man is concerned unless his life is threatened."

During the winter of 1868–69, he was employed as a sheepherder by an Irish immigrant named John Connel, known as "Smoky Jack." Connel quartered his new employee in a hovel between French Bar and Snelling, a pair of played-out mining towns on the Merced River in the Sierra foothills above the northern San Joaquin Valley. Although he had no particular interest in sheep—he would later describe sheep's brains as so meager that "an entire flock is required to make one foolish animal"—the job provided a roof over his head, if a leaky one, during his first winter in California.

Coyotes, the bane of Western sheepmen, captivated him. The reluctant shepherd described them in his journals as "the greatest of all the enemies of the California sheep-raiser, destroying many of his lambs despite his watchfulness and industry in killing them off with poison, etc." While his job required loyalty to the flock, Muir's sympathies were with the coyotes. He said, "They are beautiful animals, and, although cursed of man, are loved of God. Their sole fault is that they are fond of mutton." He routinely sent the herd dogs to chase off the predators whenever he saw them. While watching his flock one late January morning he saw "a coyote stealing from a thicket of dead weeds and earnestly watching the opportunity for a lamb. I . . . almost wished I had not seen him," he said, "that he might have had a lamb in peace."

Muir spent the next several winters in the Yosemite Valley, free of worry about the destruction wrought on sheep herds by coyotes, but witness to the destruction left in the trail of frequent avalanches. He wrote of "common, after-storm avalanches" as well as what he called "annual and century avalanches" composed of layered snow rendered unstable by alternating periods of freezing and thawing. Once unleashed, they "seldom fail to make a perfectly clean sweep, stripping off the soil as well as the trees, clearing paths two or three hundred yards wide," he wrote, "piling their uprooted trees, head downward, in rows along the sides of the gaps like lateral moraines."

In the smaller avalanches that follow most heavy winter storms in the steep-walled Yosemite Valley, he found beauty as they fell "rejoicing, to their places, whispering, thrilling like birds, or booming and roaring like thunder." He compared them to waterfalls that start high in the cliffs and slopes, when "a dull, rushing, rumbling sound is heard which rapidly increases and seems to draw nearer with appalling intensity of tone." Soon, he wrote, "the white flood comes bounding into sight over bosses and sheer places, leaping from bench to bench, spreading and narrowing and throwing off clouds of whirling dust like the spray of foaming cataracts." While short-lived when compared with waterfalls and cascades, he found avalanches very much like them "in their dress, gait, gestures, and general behavior."

One winter morning following a snowy night the ever-curious explorer, "being eager to see as many fine avalanches as possible," wallowed through waist-deep snow up an unnamed side canyon of the Yosemite Valley, occasionally sinking almost out of sight. Underestimating the difficulty, it took him all day to reach the top of the canyon. His original goal unrealized, he hoped at least to enjoy the sunset from his lofty position three thousand feet above the valley floor. That, too, proved impossible as his tramping around in the unstable snow started an avalanche and Muir was, he said, "swished down to the foot of the canyon as if by enchantment. The wallowing ascent had taken nearly all day, the descent only about a minute." Lucky for the avalanche rider, there were no cliffs or outcroppings in the canyon and by throwing himself on his back and spreading his arms and legs wide he stayed, most of the time, on the surface of the snow. When the avalanche came to a rest, he found himself "on top of the crumpled pile without a bruise or scar." He called it "a fine experience" and said his ride on "what might be called a milky way of snow-stars was the most spiritual and exhilarating of all the modes of motion. . . . Elijah's flight in a chariot of fire could hardly have been more gloriously exciting."

Another of his snowy adventures, less violent but equally dangerous, occurred in 1874. He decided he wanted to see Mount Shasta, a 14,142-foot peak in the Cascade Range in Northern California, some forty-five miles south of the Oregon border. He set out afoot from the Yosemite Valley in October heading north, and from the town of Redding walked the California-Oregon stage road. His first view of the snow-clad volcanic peak prompted this exclamation in a letter: "When I first caught sight of it over the braided folds of the Sacramento valley, I was fifty miles away and afoot, alone, and weary, yet all my blood turned to wine, and I have not been weary since." Merely looking at the mountain proved unsatisfying, however, and he determined to climb it. He outfitted himself at Sisson's Station—where the town of Mount Shasta is located today—with a blanket and food enough to last a week. While Muir gathered his supplies, proprietor Justin Sisson warned him that it was foolish to begin an ascent on the first day of November, as the snow was already deep and more was likely that time of year. "But I like snow," Muir said.

Jerome Fay—a guide and hunter employed by Sisson—accompanied him, and the pair rode horseback to the timberline where they set up camp. They arose well before dawn and the guide and the horses headed down the mountain while Muir set off uphill alone. Even bucking knee-deep snow and often sinking chest deep, he topped the mountain before midday, then a brewing storm chased him all the way back to camp, an eight-hour hike. After digging a hole on the leeward side of a jumble of lava rocks, the explorer gathered a supply of firewood and settled in to wait out the storm. It was a long wait. For four days he huddled out of the blowing snow, listening to the music of the wind, attempting to befriend a Douglas squirrel, and studying the shapes of snowflakes with a pocket magnifying glass.

Meanwhile, the worried proprietor of Sisson's Station sent the once-again mounted Fay back up the mountain on a rescue mission, leading a spare horse on the off chance the mountaineer was still alive. Reluctantly, Muir agreed to return with him. By the end of December he had made three more excursions onto Shasta's slopes, "finely nerved for the most delicate work of mountaineering both among crevasses and lava cliffs," he said. "I found some geological facts that are perfectly glorious, and some botanical ones too."

A few months later, in April 1875, another trip up Mount Shasta proved less glorious. He scaled the mountain on an expedition for the United States Coast and Geodetic Survey to take barometric readings and mark the summit with a Geodetic monument. Accompanied again by Jerome Fay, the climbers found themselves exposed on steep, bare slopes in a furious storm of freezing rain, hail, and snow driven on icy torrents of wind. Lightning and thunder, "the most tremendously loud and appalling I ever heard," Muir said, "made an almost continuous roar, stroke following stroke in quick, passionate succession, as though the mountain were being rent to its foundations and the fires of the old volcano were breaking forth again." Unable to reach the base camp downslope, the men sought shelter, such as it was, among a field of spitting fumaroles venting deadly gases, steam, and hot water from deep within the volcanic mountain. They spent a long night pinned flat to the steaming slope by howling winds, scalding on one side and freezing on the other. Even when the storm abated, darkness would not allow a descent of the dangerous mountain, so the two men suffered all the long night in the heat and cold, calling out to each other periodically, "fearing the other may be benumbed or dead."

Even in his misery, Muir said that when the sky cleared he lay there on his back, frozen and burned, and "gazed at the stars, blessed immortals of light, shining with marvelous brightness with long lance rays, near-looking and new-looking, as if never seen before." They shone, he said, "with pure and tranquil radiance." No discomfort or danger, it seems, could dampen the naturalist's enthusiasm for wild nature, at least not for long.

Seven times in his life he traveled to Alaska—the first trip in 1879 and the last in 1899—his primary motivation a fascination for the abundant glaciers there. Where glaciers meet the sea, icebergs result—ragged, rugged, often gigantic islands of floating peril for watercraft of every size and description. This menace is of particular note in Muir's case, as the customary vessels for exploring the bays, inlets, and fjords where glaciers die and icebergs are born, were tiny rowboats launched from larger seagoing ships, and, more often, fragile canoes crafted by Alaskan Indians.

Among the accounts of his journeys assembled for the book *Travels in Alaska,* was the story of a narrow escape in the iceberg-littered Glacier Bay during one of his visits there. It seems the lone explorer was paddling a canoe around the bay, assessing changes in the glaciers since his first visit in October 1879. He found "The upper half of the bay closely choked with bergs, through which it was exceedingly difficult to force a way." While searching for a sandy beach on which to camp for the night, he "came to a pack of very large bergs which loomed threateningly, offering no visible thoroughfare." He paddled around and found a "sheer-walled opening," the seeming result of a large iceberg that had split apart. He realized the danger of entering the passage, knowing that with the slightest drift of the ice the four-foot-wide gap might slam shut before he could negotiate the two hundred feet of its length. He entered nevertheless, "judging the dangers ahead might not be greater than those I had already passed." About a third of the way through, he said, "I suddenly discovered that the smooth-walled ice lane was growing narrower, and with desperate haste backed out." The close call filled him with terror, for as soon as "the bow of the canoe cleared the sheer walls they came together with a growling crunch."

He spent an uncomfortable night wedged between two boulders on a rocky shore, but felt himself rewarded for the day's danger and the night's discomfort when, in the starry sky, "magnificent upright bars of light in bright prismatic colors suddenly appeared, marching swiftly in close succession along the northern horizon from east to west . . . an auroral display very different from any I had ever before beheld." So enchanted that he lost all sense of time, he claimed he was "charmed out of mind and the blessed night circled away in measureless rejoicing enthusiasm."

Despite the danger and difficulty they represented, Muir found icebergs fascinating and beautiful, even when unaccompanied by the aurora borealis. His Alaska journals from June and July of 1890 contain a number of lyrical passages inspired by the floating spawn of his beloved glaciers:

> Icebergs tossing and drifting in the bay, grating against one another, moved by the winds on their varying faces, like sails set at every angle. Crystal to crystal in keen clashing contact.

> Dazzling in the light of noon . . . a crowded collection of this glacial jewelry, beyond description glorious!

> Ears unable to hear the still, small voice of Nature must needs hear these—the thunders of plunging, roaring icebergs.

Despite spectacular grating and clashing and crashing, the danger of icebergs is localized, and unless the explorer finds himself in the path of a pair on a collision course—as Muir had found himself—no hazard is evident. On the other hand, he knew that earthquakes wreak havoc far and wide and put at risk everyone and everything within miles of the epicenter. He knew, too, that the dangerous, violent slipping and sliding of the earth's crust created cataclysmic change in landscapes and could transform the worlds of all manner of living things.

Muir saw the Yosemite Valley forever altered when an earthquake struck at half past two in the morning on March 26, 1872. Jolted from sleep, instinctively knowing the nature of the unexpected event, he wrote of running from his cabin, certain he was going to learn something, shouting, "A noble earthquake! A noble earthquake!" The shocks were so violent and frequent that he likened the valley floor to the deck of a ship tossed by waves. He also confessed fear, believing that with such shaking the steep walls of the valley were sure to tumble. After a series of "flashing horizontal thrusts mixed with a few twists and battering explosive upheaving jolts," he said that except for a deep, distant rumbling, an eerie calm descended "as if Nature were holding her breath." Then, with a frightening roar, Eagle Rock, a formation high on the south wall of the valley, broke loose and tumbled down. "Luminous from friction," Muir described it, "an arc of glowing, passionate fire." He raced the half mile to the new talus slope and scrambled up the huge boulders even as they settled, "chafing, grating against one another, groaning, and whispering," and while fragments of granite yet rained down the cliff. The air, he said, "was filled with the odor of crushed Douglas spruces from a grove that had been mowed down and mashed like weeds." In the moonlight, he witnessed a giant cloud of dust hanging over the valley like a ceiling.

Come morning, Muir dashed about the valley to study the effects of the temblor on the streams and waterfalls, the forests, and the wildlife—robins appeared frightened, he noted, while owls seemed unconcerned. He found the Indians inhabiting the upper end of the valley anxious and anticipating death. The few white settlers in the valley at the time were gathered near Hutchings Hotel, likewise afraid, and planning to vacate the valley for the lowlands. The amateur geologist tried in vain to convince them to stay, telling them they were better off where they were, encircled by "the strength of the granite walls of our Valley home, the very best and solidest masonry in the world, and less likely to collapse than the sedimentary lowlands to which they were looking for safety." They considered him daft.

Violent aftershocks continued throughout the day, and, he said, "it was long before the Valley found perfect rest." For more than two months the quaking kept up, and so did his studies of its destructive effects. Lessons learned from what came to be called the Inyo earthquake were never forgotten, and reinforced his conclusions concerning the results of what others might consider nature at its worst: "Reading these grand mountain manuscripts through every vicissitude of heat and cold, calm and storm, upheaving volcanoes and down-grinding glaciers, we see that everything in Nature called destruction must be creation—a change from beauty to beauty."

Inventing Environmentalism

E very mythic battle includes a nemesis—an archenemy to challenge the hero—and often conflicts of more earthly proportions are also cast with similar characters. In the story of John Muir, Gifford Pinchot is usually assigned the role of villain.

The climactic moment of their story, as it appears in most commentaries on Muir, took place on September 5, 1897, in the lobby of a Seattle hotel where the two happened to cross paths. They had been associates for years, and the younger Pinchot held Muir in high esteem, crediting his wilderness-experienced friend with much of his own success as one of America's first professional foresters. Both men were early and influential participants in the birth and development of the environmental movement, although their views were not always in agreement.

Muir had stopped over in Seattle while returning from a visit to the forests of western Canada. Pinchot was in town to gather information on forest reserves in the northwestern states. As the story goes, a newspaper account of an interview with the young forester in which he opined that allowing sheep to graze in protected forests would cause little damage, had upset Muir, who had witnessed the harm sheep could cause and had come to despise the "hoofed locusts" he once tended in the Sierra. He saw Pinchot in the hotel lobby with a group of news reporters and asked him if the account was accurate. Pinchot said it was, to which the angry Muir is said to have replied, before walking away, "I don't want anything more to do with you."

The only problem with the story, after careful examination of the evidence, is that it probably did not happen as it has been handed down, and may not have occurred at all.

Muir and Pinchot first crossed paths in October 1892, just a few months after the Californian had set his signature on the founding charter establishing the Sierra Club as a recreational, educational, and political organization that he would serve, as president, for the rest of his life. The two men spent a few autumn days that year hiking through upstate New York's Adirondack Mountains with the mutual friend who introduced them. Pinchot, born to wealth and privilege in 1865, was then twenty-seven, a graduate of Yale University, and had recently returned from Europe where he studied forestry, as no American university offered such a program. He had so enjoyed the Adirondack trek that he sent Muir a hunting knife as a gift to commemorate their meeting.

The following summer, June 1893, they met again at a formal dinner at Pinchot's parents' home in the elegant Gramercy Park neighborhood of New York City. The wealthy New Yorkers were familiar with Muir's literary work and reputation and invited him to their home while he was in town awaiting the departure of a ship to Europe. The rustic mountaineer entertained his upscale audience—along with servants lurking unobtrusively within earshot, he said—with tales of his wilderness adventures, including the popular story of the dog Stickeen's harrowing escapade on an Alaskan glacier. The elder Pinchots enjoyed Muir's company and invited him for several other visits while in the city.

He, too, found the company agreeable—especially that of Gifford. "Nothing in all my trip gave me greater pleasure than finding you a Young Man devoting yourself to the study of World Forestry amid the world of commerce," he wrote to Pinchot. He encouraged his new friend to get out alone in the forests, to learn from the trees firsthand. The forester took the advice, and wrote that, "In a small way I have tried your plan of going alone, and was off for four days by myself." The veteran explorer sent praise in return: "Happy man. You will never regret a single day spent thus," he wrote, adding that he regretted not being able to join him on his walks. They got the chance to walk together a few years later, however, courtesy of the National Forestry Commission.

The commission was the brainchild of Charles Sargent, another influential figure in the early days of environmentalism. Muir had met him through *Century* magazine associate editor Robert Underwood Johnson, during the same 1893 New York City layover that had found the traveler dining at the Pinchot residence. Sargent, born to a wealthy Boston family in 1841, was, among his many other accomplishments, founder and director of Harvard's Arnold Arboretum.

By 1895, it was obvious to many Americans with an interest in forest land—including Sargent—that even the land set aside by the Forest Reserve Act of 1891 was in poor condition and growing worse. While the land had been set aside, no laws or regulations had been enacted for its use, or finances provided for its care or maintenance. As a result, an audit by the Public Land Service revealed that unrestricted mining, illegal logging, unauthorized grazing, and related burning had lately picked $37 million from the public pocket. The Harvard horticulturist suggested assembling a panel of experts to survey the situation and recommend ways to ensure the forests would remain vital and lasting. The editor Johnson and the upstart forester Pinchot aided in the planning and development of the idea. Johnson had written Muir of the plan and was told in reply that "The Sargent plan of salvation of trees will prove, I think, a glorious reformation and make the pine needles tingle with joy."

Congress, however, influenced by moneyed lumber and livestock interests, saw no reason to appoint such a commission, so Charles Sargent asked Johnson of *Century* to wield his influence in Washington to engineer a clever alternative to congressional action. The editor visited the secretary of the interior, explained the plan, and asked the secretary to request the National Academy of Sciences, as an advisor to the government, to establish the commission.

This was accomplished in 1896. Sargent was appointed chairman, Pinchot secretary, and five others were named commission members. Because of concern for his health, Muir asked to serve the commission as an advisor rather than an official member, believing he could still be influential in an advisory role. Johnson was also able to persuade the chairman of the House Appropriations Committee to commit $25,000 to cover expenses for the commission. The service of the commissioners was voluntary.

Muir's health improved and when the commission departed from Chicago on July 5, he was with them. Along with most of the commissioners—others would join up along the way—he traveled to the Black Hills of South Dakota, Wyoming's Bighorn Mountains, the Bitterroot range in Idaho and Montana, the Cascades in Washington and Oregon, then California's Sierra Nevada, San Bernardino, and San Jacinto mountains, finishing up the tour at the Grand Canyon in Arizona Territory. Muir and Pinchot found plenty of opportunities to hike together as the commission went about its work. At Grand Canyon, the two left the group to explore along the south rim, studying the richness of the desert rocks and plants. Rather than return to the hotel, they bedded down among the juniper and pine trees at the edge of the gorge where they talked through the night.

Although everyone on the commission witnessed widespread abuse and destruction of the forest reserves, a difference of opinion emerged during the travels and intensified during the preparation of the commission's report. One faction, headed by Sargent, lobbied for preservation and protection of the forests at the expense of every other use, with military patrols by cavalry troops enforcing compliance. The other opinion, promoted by Pinchot, wanted civil-service rangers rather than military patrols, and policies that permitted legitimate and regulated use of the land by miners, loggers, and stockmen. Sargent came to view Pinchot as an inexperienced upstart who lacked proper appreciation for trees, while the younger man believed the chairman's hardened views were unrealistic and outmoded.

Muir's sympathies and support were in Sargent's camp, even though his views on maintaining forests in pristine condition were not as extreme. Firmly opposed to allowing sheep on the land under any circumstances—based on years of watching Sierra forests overgrazed to desolation and sheepmen burning off trees in the hope of establishing new range— he believed that responsible logging was a legitimate enterprise. As he wrote later in "The American Forests," one of a series of essays published in *The Atlantic Monthly* in 1898, and in the 1901 book, *Our National Parks,* "The remnant protected will yield plenty of timber, a perennial harvest for every right use, without further diminution of its area."

The disagreements resulted in a compromise report with which no member of the commission was happy. Military patrols were recommended, but only until civilian rangers could be hired, organized, and trained. Thirteen new forest reserves and two new national parks—Mount Rainier and Grand Canyon—were recommended.

President Grover Cleveland received a preliminary draft of the report as his days in office dwindled, and he took the unprecedented step of placing, by executive order, twenty-two million additional acres of forest into the recommended reserves. Widespread protest resulted, especially in the West where the reserves were located. Although the presidential order said nothing about how the reserves were to be regulated, logging, mining, and grazing interests perceived a threat and went to work immediately to have the action overturned.

The work of the commission was effectively set aside with the arrival of the William McKinley administration, and through behind-the-scenes political maneuvering in Congress when the commission's final report was submitted. On June 4, 1897, Congress passed a watered-down Forest Management Act that delayed the preservation of most of the forest reserves Cleveland had announced, failed to formalize regulation of the forests, and unleashed a wave of rush and ruin by land-grabbers and speculators. With the Act, battle lines were drawn for future skirmishes on many fronts—political conflicts, commercial clashes, disagreements in the budding environmental movement, even quarrels between Muir and Pinchot.

Muir's despair in watching politicians, bureaucrats, and money interests dilute the recommendations of the Forest Commission found voice in his "The American Forests" essay in the August 1897 *Atlantic Monthly*. "Any fool can destroy trees. They cannot run away; and if they could, they would still be destroyed—chased and hunted down as long as fun or a dollar could be got out of their bark hides," he wrote. "God has cared for these trees, saved them from drought, disease, avalanches, and a thousand straining, leveling tempests and floods; but he cannot save them from fools,—only Uncle Sam can do that." But, it seemed, Uncle Sam would not.

Even as the magazine article was generating outrage among many citizens concerned with the fate of their American forests, the author was studying the woods in western Canada with Charles Sargent. Sargent's opinions of commission secretary Pinchot had not softened and had, in fact, intensified during the preparation of the commission report. When Pinchot was appointed forestry agent for the Department of the Interior, Sargent had expressed his unhappiness. Muir, on the other hand, seemed pleased at the development, both for Pinchot personally and for the "grand work" he could do with the position. It was an uncomfortable place for Muir to be, between the combative Sargent and Pinchot, for he liked them both and saw much to agree with in each man's views.

Still, fresh out of the woods and Sargent's company that September morning in the Seattle hotel lobby, it is possible that strong words from the chairman of the Forest Commission about its secretary were ringing in Muir's ears. Did that echo contribute to his alleged notorious encounter with Pinchot? Or, was the encounter exaggerated—even fabricated—in the creation of an environmental movement myth?

Pinchot biographer Char Miller carefully researched the event and surrounding documentation, and questions the accuracy of the popular account. There is a question of timing. Pinchot's diary verifies a meeting with Muir on September 5, but under different circumstances. After lunch with a friend from the United States Geological Survey, he wrote that he "met John Muir in the lobby. Spent the afternoon with these two. Much delighted to see Mr. Muir again." The entry went on to record dinner with the same companions, followed by church attendance, an interview with a newspaper reporter, "then more later with Muir."

There is no mention in Pinchot's diary of any disagreement with his old friend over sheep grazing during their time together September 5. If his account is accurate, the forester was not even interviewed for the story in question until late that day. The newspaper article, when it appeared the morning of

September 6—the day *after* the men met at the hotel—included a brief statement that "Pasturage may also be permitted by the secretary under suitable rules and regulations." Chronology, then, renders the popular rendition of the argument impossible.

Dates are easily confused, however, so the anachronism could be an innocent mistake. Muir's ship set sail from Seattle at eight o'clock in the morning on September 6, requiring him to be aboard hours earlier. An early-morning encounter—very early—would have been possible, but there are other difficulties. According to biographer Miller, the recollection of the incident, which has been passed down through the years, was that of Muir's friend and Sierra Club secretary, William E. Colby, who claimed to have witnessed the encounter. His account surrounded the quarrel in the hotel lobby with a group of newspaper reporters. Yet none of those journalists bothered to record the confrontation for readers or for posterity, or report it in their newspapers, then or later.

Most telling of all, perhaps, is what happened to the relationship between the two after the clash in which Muir reportedly said to Pinchot, "I don't want anything more to do with you." In a December 1897 letter to "My Dear Pinchot" he wrote, "I was very glad to get your cheery hopeful forest letter," and complained that the General Land Office had "thrown open the Oregon Reserves to sheepmen and sheep." So, while the onetime shepherd had grown to distrust stock raisers' ability to control themselves or their herds where public lands were concerned, Pinchot's biographer Char Miller believed that Muir—even though he disagreed and disapproved—recognized a distinction between Pinchot's desire to allow grazing if properly regulated, and the wide-open approach of the Land Office. "I shall be glad to hear how you succeed in your forest plans," he wrote to close the letter.

Whether the clash happened as popularized or not, it marked a split in the fledgling environmental movement. The desires of Charles Sargent and others, including Muir, to prohibit virtually all grazing, logging, mining, and most other kinds of development of wild lands came to be labeled "preservationist," while the approach Pinchot championed, allowing these kinds of activities so long as they were regulated to prevent permanent damage, would be called the "conservationist" view. The gap was a narrow one then, however, and Muir and Pinchot, the representatives of the opposing camps and diverging views, remained cordial for a time. Pinchot continued to ask Muir for advice and counsel, with increasingly less deference, however, and valued his experience and opinions. Each recognized the other as occupying a useful and influential position in the cause of forest protection. They realized their differences were trivial when compared to the intentions of their common enemies in the battle for the forests, the well-heeled interests who lobbied endlessly for unrestricted and unregulated access to grass, lumber, minerals, and land.

Already firmly entrenched in government service since his 1897 appointment as forestry agent for the Department of the Interior, Pinchot's association with the national forests was solidified when he was put in charge of the Department of Agriculture's Division of Forestry in 1898. In the new role he was saddled with attempting to balance management of the forests against a number of conflicting interests. The press of work forced him to decline several invitations from his mountaineer friend to go exploring, but Pinchot finally broke away for a five-day jaunt with Muir in the Sierra in 1899, which included a visit to an ancient sequoia grove whose existence was threatened by the designs of loggers. Pinchot wrote after returning home that the trip was "one of the brightest spots in my year."

Meanwhile, Muir also maintained a friendly relationship with Charles Sargent. The two set out in 1898, the year after their tour of western Canadian forests, for the woods of the southeastern American states, sometimes crossing the path of Muir's 1867 thousand-mile walk. They launched a world tour together in 1903, preceded by a stay in Brookline, Massachusetts, at Sargent's home. The visit was celebrated with a formal dinner for which Muir, at age sixty-five, donned his first tuxedo.

Pinchot headed the Forestry Division for twelve years under three presidents, until relieved of duty in 1910 for insubordination, owing to his claims that the William Howard Taft administration was abandoning principles of conservation. The forester would twice serve as governor of Pennsylvania and teach at his namesake Pinchot School of Forestry at Yale University.

But it was before all that, during the presidential administration of Theodore Roosevelt, that he played his final, significant role in the life of Muir. They found themselves on opposite sides of Yosemite's gaping Hetch Hetchy gorge, their friendship stretched thin as they engaged in a desperate tug-of-war for the conservation-minded president's favor and the future of the valley.

Appointment with the President

hen William McKinley died from an assassin's bullet September 14, 1901, Ohio senator and Republican power broker Mark Hanna remarked, "Now look, that damn cowboy is president of the United States."

"That damn cowboy" was Theodore Roosevelt, twenty-sixth president and, at age forty-two, the youngest man ever sworn to that office.

Throughout his political career, Roosevelt had been a reformer who challenged privilege and patronage and as a result, often ruffled the feathers of the conservative laissez-faire Republicans in his party who were comfortable with and profited from the status quo. His nomination for vice president had been, in fact, engineered by powerful New York politicians who wanted to rid themselves of a man they considered a meddlesome governor and uncontrollable radical.

In an attempt to calm fears in the party, Roosevelt kept

most members of his predecessor's cabinet in place. In other ways, he offended the political machine. Southern politicians were infuriated, for example, when he invited emancipated slave and educator Booker T. Washington to dinner at the White House. He sided with mine workers in a strike, upsetting powerful mine owners. Others were disturbed when he forced the breakup of a monopolistic railroad trust.

The new president's dissatisfaction with business-as-usual extended to the nation's natural resources. His ranching days in Dakota Territory had taught him the importance of water and range conservation in the arid West, and he viewed minerals and forest resources as public assets that deserved protection against exploitation by private interests. Many of his evolving ideas on woodland management would be influenced by Gifford Pinchot, the government's chief forester, who became one of his most trusted advisors. He would also look elsewhere for information and advice, however, including personal visits to wilderness lands and seeking out the views of authorities wherever he found them, one of whom was John Muir.

It happened that Roosevelt knew lobbyist and *Century* magazine editor Robert Underwood Johnson, whose influence had been instrumental in the passage of the 1891 Forest Reserve Act. After meeting with the president early in 1903 and learning he planned to visit California and the West, Johnson urged Roosevelt to call on Muir for a guided tour of Yosemite. The president, familiar with the mountaineer's writings, took the advice and extended the invitation.

Muir accepted, delaying the start of an around-the-world expedition with friend and Harvard horticulturist Charles Sargent. In postponing the departure date, he wrote that "an influential man from Washington wants to make a trip to the Sierra with me," and opined that the time so spent might prove beneficial to the forests they both loved. Sargent, while he consented to the delay, doubted the value of a meeting with the "influential man," believing Roosevelt to be "too much under the influence of that creature Pinchot," whom he had disliked since their service together on the National Forestry Commission of 1896.

Even though Johnson believed the president's visit and the guide's persuasive power could positively affect the fate of forests in general, he and Muir had a more specific objective in mind: saving the Yosemite Valley. Its present troubles had their roots in the actions of an earlier president, Abraham Lincoln, who had signed legislation in 1864 that set aside the unique valley "for public use, resort, and recreation," then turned it over to the State of California for administration. However, the forests and mountains surrounding the valley went unprotected at the time and were ragged and tattered from overgrazing and intensive logging. So, the editor and writer had teamed up in 1889 to fight for the protection of the Sierra surrounding Yosemite Valley by having it set aside as a national park. The mission was accomplished and Congress created Yosemite National Park on October 1, 1890, despite bitter and determined opposition. With the possibility of a sympathetic president now in power, the preservation-minded Muir and Johnson determined the time was right to have control of Yosemite Valley—still a state park but surrounded by the national park—taken back from California and placed under federal control.

They were helped by the fact that the state legislature and the commissioners they appointed to control and protect the valley had accomplished none of the task. The Yosemite Valley was out of control and unprotected, the victim of criminal neglect. Barns, stables, stores, shops, saloons, shacks, sheds, fences, fields, pigpens, and chicken coops littered the valley floor; many of the trees that had once grown there had been felled and hastily sawn to lumber; hundreds of horses grazed at will, denuding the once-verdant meadows and trampling what they did not eat into the dust. It was such a malodorous mess, Muir said, that "Some of the stink I'm afraid has got into the pores of the rocks, even."

Efforts had been under way in the California statehouse since 1897 to free the valley of state control, and even though the idea was politically unpopular it had slowly gained support and was still being pursued by some members of the legislature. Muir saw an opportunity to use his time alone with Roosevelt to convince the administration to apply pressure from Washington in favor of federal control. Since the president specified, "I do not want anyone but you, and I want to drop politics absolutely for four days, and just be out in the open with you," Muir realized he would have a private audience and intended to put it to good use. Apparently he believed that lobbying for the removal of Yosemite Valley from state control did not qualify as "politics," so need not be "dropped."

The usually unkempt naturalist bought a new three-piece suit for the occasion, stuck a sprig of incense cedar in the lapel, as was his custom, and on the evening of May 15, 1903, boarded the presidential train at Oakland, California. Morning found the party more than one hundred and fifty miles south and west, across the San Joaquin Valley at a whistle-stop town called Raymond. During the more than thirty miles by stagecoach through the Sierra foothills to the Mariposa Sequoia Grove, Muir shared a seat with the president and George Pardee, governor of California, and pointed out sights along the way while pointing out all the reasons California should return Yosemite Valley to federal control. The entourage toured the grove in the late afternoon, after which Roosevelt sent his handlers and hangers-on to the hotel at Wawona where an evening reception was in the making.

The president, however, stayed at the grove where he intended to sleep out among the trees with Muir. Two Yosemite rangers were the only others in the camp, there to cook supper and ensure the president's privacy. Already aware of his host's skill with the written word, Roosevelt soon learned the man's voice was a mightier—and more prolific—instrument than his pen, and at the end of Muir's oratory on the Yosemite Valley, the president promised to sign a bill returning the place to federal oversight if Congress would send him one.

At bedtime, Muir arranged heaps of evergreen boughs for mattresses, upon which the president spread his unusual bed— a stack of blankets some forty deep, into which he could burrow at any depth he chose to provide the desired mix of cushion and cover. Roosevelt later described the giant rust-colored trunks towering over them in the firelight as "columns of a vaster and more beautiful cathedral than was ever conceived by any human architect."

By six-thirty in the morning, the campers had breakfasted and were in the saddle. The guides led the president, at his request, on a back trail into the wilderness to avoid the Wawona hotel and the distractions of the entourage there. Through occasional deep snow and bitter winds they made their way to

Glacier Point, a dramatic overlook on the south rim of Yosemite Valley, and pitched camp in a protected cove nearby. "Now this is bully!" Roosevelt said of the experience, and in the morning, when he awoke under an additional blanket of four inches of snow, he said, "This is bullier yet! I wouldn't miss this for anything."

Between these exclamations, he and Muir talked at great length (most likely considerable depth and width as well, given that both men were famous talkers) about conservation, preservation, protection, parks, watersheds, and scenery. Even glaciers entered into the discussions, as the amateur geologist explained to the president his theories of how the mountains around and the valley below them were sculpted by rivers of ice.

The two men shook off the snow and kept an appointment with the expedition's official photographer. There was no shortage of photogenic backdrops from atop Glacier Point: Nevada Falls, Vernal Falls, and Little Yosemite below; or the smooth top and sheer face of Half Dome looming almost near enough to touch; the course of Tenaya Creek through polished, rippling granite; North Dome; El Capitan. The most famous snap of that day, however, placed Roosevelt and Muir on Overhang Rock, from which a 3,200-foot drop to the valley below was a mere two steps in three directions. Across the main gorge behind the pair, just to the right of the president, the misty ribbon of Upper Yosemite Falls tumbles off its sheer cliff, with every inch of its 1,433 free fall visible in the frame.

In the photo, the president's stern face, spectacles, and mustache are familiar, his high-crowned Western hat less so. His neck is wrapped in a knotted scarf, his coat ends just below his hips, his riding breeches tucked into high-top boots. Muir, at the president's left in three-quarter view, stands stiffly with hands clasped behind his back. A stem of greenery dangles from the lapel of his suit jacket. The lean, weathered face is topped by a fedora and a full beard hangs beneath. His gaze seems fixed in the middle distance.

After the shutter clicked, they made their way down off the point and into the Little Yosemite Valley, where the pair continued sightseeing and stopped for lunch along the Merced River. Near Nevada Falls they found a waiting crowd but the president wanted more time alone with his experienced tour guide and had them sent away. Several other groups were stationed along the trails leading to the main valley, all hoping for a look at the former Rough Rider, and Roosevelt acknowledged their presence with a wave of his hand but little more. The mounted admirers fell in behind Muir and Roosevelt, forming a parade until the president reined up and sent the followers on down the trail, saying he did not want to "lead a procession."

The crowds grew larger and more frequent as they approached the valley proper, however, and Roosevelt realized an obligation to his constituents and so stopped at Sentinel Bridge to mingle with the throng, all smiles and excitement as he answered questions about his time in the mountains with John Muir. "This is the day of my life, one that I will always remember with pleasure. Just think of where I was last night," he said, pointing to the top of the looming canyon wall toward Glacier Point. "Up there."

The entourage of politicians and promoters had arranged a party and reception for the president, to be concluded with an impressive display of fireworks, but again, Roosevelt disappointed them. He departed with Muir for another quiet camp, this one at Bridal Veil meadow, a verdant clearing tucked against the cliffs of Yosemite Valley's south wall near the delicate Bridal Veil waterfall. The crowd followed, trailing after Muir and Roosevelt, some afoot, some horseback, others in buggies and wagons. This time, the weary president ordered the rangers to send the admirers away. "Those people annoy me," he said. "Can you get rid of them?" They could. The now-fast friends spent their third night together, again discussing the fate of the forests with Roosevelt's tales of adventure thrown in to flavor the conversation.

A stagecoach trip to Wawona for lunch, then on to Raymond, and a train ride back to Oakland brought their time together to an end, but their few days in the Sierra would have lasting effects. Eventually, the State of California's holdings in Yosemite Valley would be turned over to the federal government due, in part, to Muir's influence with the president and Governor Pardee on the trip. But the issue was not resolved easily. States' rights, state pride, the economic interests of valley concessionaires were impediments to the transfer among California politicians. Against these interests, and with support from members of the Sierra Club, Muir orchestrated an intensive lobbying effort when the legislature gathered in January 1905. He made public speeches and buttonholed lawmakers and journalists seeking support. In the end, it took behind-the-scenes maneuvering by lobbyists for the Southern Pacific Railroad to engineer passage of the legislation. Railroad men were still influential in California politics, and they, at the insistence of Edward H. Harriman, who controlled the Southern Pacific, lined up the necessary votes. The railroad baron acted after being persuaded to do so by his unlikely friend, John Muir.

Even with passage of the bill by the California legislature, opposition in both houses of Congress in Washington delayed the absorption of Yosemite Valley into the national park around it for another year. When Roosevelt finally kept his word to Muir and signed the bill, Muir wrote of the victory to Robert Underwood Johnson: "Sound the timbrel and let every Yosemite tree and stream rejoice!"

Meantime, the president continued efforts on behalf of forest preservation, taking an initial action in what would become a lengthy and widespread effort to save pristine forests. This was an executive order extending the Sierra Forest Reserve north to Mount Shasta, as recommended by his newest advisor, John Muir. By 1907, pressure from Western congressmen, in whose states most of the protected forests were located, resulted in legislation to prevent the president from setting aside any more forestland in six designated Western states without congressional approval. The action slowed Roosevelt but did not stop him. Between passage of the law and its effective date, he issued proclamations ordering seventy-five million acres of forest preserved by expanding some existing national forests and creating other new ones. Before leaving office in 1909, he had more than tripled the amount of land in national forests, from forty-three million acres to more than one hundred and fifty million.

While Muir was pleased with the new and expanded forests, his enthusiasm was dampened by the influence of Gifford Pinchot in their management. The government forester's philosophy of administering national forests for economic values such as timber production and grazing, as well as the intrinsic values Muir held dear, was suspect in the preservationist's eyes. Roosevelt sought and valued advice from each man, and must go dry unless Hetch Hetchy Yosemite is drowned is ridiculous."

In April 1906, a little more than a year after this correspondence, the issue took on increasing importance when a horrific earthquake rocked San Francisco. The temblor caused extensive damage across the peninsula, but the fires it caused proved the more destructive force. Flames raced along the waterfront and up and down the many hills, leveling block after block of the crowded city. Through it all, firefighters looked on helplessly— the quake had snapped the water mains and no water was available to fight the fires.

While the dry pipes were the result of earthquake damage rather than a shortage of water, James Phelan, no longer mayor but still active in civic affairs, did not hesitate to place a portion of the blame on the absence of a dam and reservoir at Hetch Hetchy. The claim was absurd, since the vast amount of work required would not have allowed Tuolumne River water to reach the city by 1906 even if the earliest request to build the dam had been approved. Still, the claim was widely believed and accelerated efforts to bring Yosemite water to San Francisco. In 1907, Pinchot encouraged the city to file another request, assuring them that the newly appointed secretary of the interior would view it favorably.

President Theodore Roosevelt admired both Muir and Pinchot and relied on their advice concerning environmental policy, but while influenced by both men, he made his own decisions. Muir reminded the president that he had vowed to protect the national parks from the very kind of exploitation represented by the endeavor to dam Hetch Hetchy. Pinchot's hope was that "in the regeneration of San Francisco its people may be able to make provision for a water supply from the Yosemite National Park," and that he would "stand ready to render any assistance which lies in my power."

After weighing all sides and considering all the evidence, the president suggested that the two men get together and come up with a workable solution. Pinchot dutifully journeyed to California and spent a day meeting with his friend-turned-foe. The forester admitted that he had never seen the Valley and was surprised, according to Muir, "to learn how important a part of the Yosemite National Park the Hetch Hetchy really is." They parted with the understanding that the Interior Department would not act until Muir could lay out his arguments in writing.

The explorer's subsequent report did not convince the interior secretary, however, nor did it change Pinchot's mind. "I believe that the highest possible use" for the Hetch Hetchy Valley, he told Roosevelt, "would be to supply pure water to a great center of population." The president informed Muir of the recommendation and his intention to endorse it, primarily because of popular support for the idea and a comparative lack of opposition. "I have been in the disagreeable position of seeming to interfere with the development of the State for the sake of keeping a valley, which apparently hardly anyone wanted to have kept."

Roosevelt did, however, attempt to soften the blow. The city's request included both the Hetch Hetchy site and Lake Eleanor, the latter outside the park's boundaries. The president recommended that approval for the Hetch Hetchy dam be withdrawn and only Lake Eleanor be developed. The interior secretary did not believe he could take such drastic action, however, and offered the compromise that the dam in the national park could be built, but only *after* the Lake Eleanor site was fully developed. Too, rather than give San Francisco unconditional authorization to build the dam, the permit required congressional approval and could be revoked. It was a victory for the city, but a limited one, and the effective result was merely to delay a firm decision one way or another. The president urged Muir to use the lull to drum up public opposition to the dam, at which point he, too, would sustain the preservationist's position. "I would not have any difficulty at all if, as you say, nine tenths of the citizens took ground against the Hetch Hetchy project."

The Interior Department granted San Francisco the revocable permit in May 1908, and Muir took the president's advice and, with help from the Sierra Club and other preservationists, mounted a publicity campaign and lobbying effort. Although the proposed compromise effectively delayed the damming of the Tuolumne River at Hetch Hetchy for the time being and well into the future, Muir believed that if the need for a dam was not urgent, then permission to build it should not be granted at all. The publicity effort generated enough support to make Congress question the permit and no action was taken, nor would it be for the remainder of Roosevelt's term.

The strained relationship between Muir and Pinchot resulted in a public slight against the elder statesman of the wilderness by his onetime protégé. In May 1908, Roosevelt convened a Governors' Conference on Conservation at the White House. Although the conference's purpose was to celebrate the president's unprecedented contributions to the cause of conservation, it was

Pinchot who organized and orchestrated the event, and his views on the use of natural resources dominated the meetings. Forty-four governors from states and territories were joined by hundreds of government officials and experts from related fields.

Absent from the affair were John Muir and his friend Charles Sargent. Both were widely recognized experts in forestry, both had the benefit of decades of experience, both had firsthand knowledge of woodlands in every region of the country and had seen and understood the challenges the trees faced, and both had informed opinions about protecting them.

Unfortunately, neither man was in the good graces of the conference organizer. Pinchot and Sargent had developed a mutual dislike during their service together on the National Forestry Commission in 1896. Pinchot's relationship with Muir, already stretched thin by their diverging views on forest management, was at the breaking point, if not already broken, by the Hetch Hetchy controversy. With the exclusion of Muir and Sargent and others of like mind, the preservationist position had no voice at the meetings, either at the lectern or in the audience.

The conference's stated purpose of commemorating the Roosevelt administration's protection of the environment left attendees with the impression that the president subscribed to the Pinchot camp's philosophy. The "conservationist" view espoused managing natural resources on public land to provide the greatest good for the greatest number of people for the longest time. Scenic beauty, environmental integrity, or other intrinsic values merited only secondary consideration. Yet during his final tempered the influence of one with the other. Then, being persistently independent, the president would find his own way toward consensus through the thick woods of conflicting interests.

Not long after his Yosemite trip, Roosevelt found himself in the midst of a growing controversy that would polarize Muir and Pinchot: the desire of the city of San Francisco to dam the Tuolumne River and use the Hetch Hetchy Valley in Yosemite National Park as a reservoir for drinking water. Muir would win a battle while Roosevelt remained president, but the war for the Hetch Hetchy would ultimately outlast his term in office.

Never again would the former-cowboy president of the United States and the former-sheepherder president of the Sierra Club find occasion to enjoy one another's companionship around a wilderness campfire, each vying to get the next word in edgewise. They would not relive the Sierra experience, but in a sense they did not have to, for it had been the experience of a lifetime for both men.

"Good-bye, John. Come and see me in Washington. I've had the time of my life," the Rough Rider told his new friend at the end of their journey. For his part, Muir said that he "never before had met so interesting, hearty, and manly a companion" as Roosevelt. "I fairly fell in love with him," he said.

Hetch Hetchy Be Dammed

Since 1849, when San Francisco was overrun by gold-fevered would-be miners and grew from a dilapidated tent village into a bustling, makeshift city, one governmental fear was constant: running short of drinking water. City fathers cast about continuously for a source of water that would free them from the grip of the Spring Valley Water Company, a private monopoly that tied up the water supply and distribution systems and relentlessly gouged San Francisco residents for the privilege of purchasing this life necessity. Upstream from the city by the bay lay the well-watered western slope of the Sierra, and repeated studies and surveys there, commissioned by San Francisco politicians, revealed the Tuolumne River system as the most likely candidate for providing the city an unfettered water supply.

Tuolumne River water poured into the southern extremes of San Francisco Bay after flowing almost due west across the San Joaquin Valley, rolling past Modesto on the way. In the Sierra foothills, the outflow of Lake Eleanor augmented the river. A few miles inside the border of Yosemite National Park, the river emerged from a narrow gap cut through high, steep cliffs. Behind the gap lay Hetch Hetchy Valley, a relatively flat, three-mile-long gorge walled by tall cliffs. In all ways, Hetch Hetchy was a miniature Yosemite, differing only in scale. The name came from the Indian word for a kind of grass that grew in the valley, from which the natives would harvest seeds that were an important part of their diet.

The City of San Francisco set its sights on Hetch Hetchy, and this is where Muir would wage his last battle for the sanctity of the Yosemite, the Sierra, and the intrinsic value of nature. The fight was long and bitter, the combatants were many, and the chronology is complex.

The first shot fired came from the city at the turn of the twentieth century with such stealth and subterfuge that those who would someday form the opposition were not even aware that the war for the Hetch Hetchy had already begun. James D. Phelan, mayor of San Francisco, was convinced that the Tuolumne was the most feasible of all available options for securing the water the city needed, and a dam at Hetch Hetchy was the way to get it. The problem lay in the fact that the river was not available, as the gap where it would be dammed, and the valley where the water would be impounded, were inside the boundaries of Yosemite National Park, and thus out of bounds. The enterprising mayor convinced one of California's congressional representatives to introduce seemingly benign legislation allowing "for domestic, public, or other beneficial uses," the construction and maintenance of canals, pipelines, tunnels, and other means of conveying water through national parks. The Right of Way Act passed without discussion or debate in February 1901, and in October, Mayor Phelan quietly applied at the Stockton Land Office for reservoir rights at Hetch Hetchy and Lake Eleanor.

No one paid much attention at the time, and Muir would not know of these machinations until 1905 when he learned of them secondhand from Gifford Pinchot.

In 1898, Pinchot had been appointed head of the Division of Forestry, then a part of the Department of Agriculture. The bureaucratic position required him to juggle conflicting interests, and since the idea that forests should be managed for multiple use—conserved, rather than preserved—increasingly dominated his beliefs, he came to the opinion that the Hetch Hetchy dam should be built. In 1903 and 1905, San Francisco had quietly petitioned the Interior Department for permission to build the dam in the national park, but had been turned down despite Pinchot's assurances that damming the Tuolumne at Hetch Hetchy would not "injure the National Park or detract from it beauties or natural grandeur."

"I cannot believe Pinchot, if he really knows the valley, has made any such statements," Muir said when told about the situation. He wrote to the forester for clarification, and got it. While sympathetic with "the extreme desirability of preserving the Hetch Hetchy in its original beauty," that desirability must be balanced against the need for water in San Francisco, Pinchot said. Muir fired off a reply, probably his last letter to an old friend whose views had diverged from his own. He pointed out that other, admittedly more expensive, sources of water were available, and that "The idea that San Francisco must go dry unless Hetch Hetchy Yosemite is drowned is ridiculous."

In April 1906, a little more than a year after this correspondence, the issue took on increasing importance when a horrific earthquake rocked San Francisco. The temblor caused extensive damage across the peninsula, but the fires it caused proved the more destructive force. Flames raced along the waterfront and up and down the many hills, leveling block after block of the crowded city. Through it all, firefighters looked on helplessly—the quake had snapped the water mains and no water was available to fight the fires.

While the dry pipes were the result of earthquake damage rather than a shortage of water, James Phelan, no longer mayor but still active in civic affairs, did not hesitate to place a portion of the blame on the absence of a dam and reservoir at Hetch Hetchy. The claim was absurd, since the vast amount of work required would not have allowed Tuolumne River water to reach the city by 1906 even if the earliest request to build the dam had been approved. Still, the claim was widely believed and accelerated efforts to bring Yosemite water to San Francisco. In 1907, Pinchot encouraged the city to file another request, assuring them that the newly appointed secretary of the interior would view it favorably.

President Theodore Roosevelt admired both Muir and Pinchot and relied on their advice concerning environmental policy, but while influenced by both men, he made his own decisions. Muir reminded the president that he had vowed to protect the national parks from the very kind of exploitation represented by the endeavor to dam Hetch Hetchy. Pinchot's hope was that "in the regeneration of San Francisco its people may be able to make provision for a water supply from the Yosemite National Park," and that he would "stand ready to render any assistance which lies in my power."

After weighing all sides and considering all the evidence, the president suggested that the two men get together and come up with a workable solution. Pinchot dutifully journeyed to California and spent a day meeting with his friend-turned-foe. The forester admitted that he had never seen the Valley and was surprised, according to Muir, "to learn how important a part of the Yosemite National Park the Hetch Hetchy really is." They parted with the understanding that the Interior Department would not act until Muir could lay out his arguments in writing.

The explorer's subsequent report did not convince the interior secretary, however, nor did it change Pinchot's mind. "I believe that the highest possible use" for the Hetch Hetchy Valley, he told Roosevelt, "would be to supply pure water to a great center of population." The president informed Muir of the recommendation and his intention to endorse it, primarily because of popular support for the idea and a comparative lack of opposition. "I have been in the disagreeable position of seeming to interfere with the development of the State for the sake of keeping a valley, which apparently hardly anyone wanted to have kept."

Roosevelt did, however, attempt to soften the blow. The city's request included both the Hetch Hetchy site and Lake Eleanor, the latter outside the park's boundaries. The president recommended that approval for the Hetch Hetchy dam be withdrawn and only Lake Eleanor be developed. The interior secretary did not believe he could take such drastic action, however, and offered the compromise that the dam in the national park could be built, but only *after* the Lake Eleanor site was fully developed. Too, rather than give San Francisco unconditional authorization to build the dam, the permit required congressional approval and could be revoked. It was a victory for the city, but a limited one, and the effective result was merely to delay a firm decision one way or another. The president urged Muir to use the lull to drum up public opposition to the dam, at which point he, too, would sustain the preservationist's position. "I would not have any difficulty at all if, as you say, nine tenths of the citizens took ground against the Hetch Hetchy project."

The Interior Department granted San Francisco the revocable permit in May 1908, and Muir took the president's advice and, with help from the Sierra Club and other preservationists, mounted a publicity campaign and lobbying effort. Although the proposed compromise effectively delayed the damming of the Tuolumne River at Hetch Hetchy for the time being and well into the future, Muir believed that if the need for a dam was not urgent, then permission to build it should not be granted at all. The publicity effort generated enough support to make Congress question the permit and no action was taken, nor would it be for the remainder of Roosevelt's term.

The strained relationship between Muir and Pinchot resulted in a public slight against the elder statesman of the wilderness by his onetime protégé. In May 1908, Roosevelt convened a Governors' Conference on Conservation at the White House. Although the conference's purpose was to celebrate the president's unprecedented contributions to the cause of conservation, it was

Pinchot who organized and orchestrated the event, and his views on the use of natural resources dominated the meetings. Forty-four governors from states and territories were joined by hundreds of government officials and experts from related fields.

Absent from the affair were John Muir and his friend Charles Sargent. Both were widely recognized experts in forestry, both had the benefit of decades of experience, both had firsthand knowledge of woodlands in every region of the country and had seen and understood the challenges the trees faced, and both had informed opinions about protecting them.

Unfortunately, neither man was in the good graces of the conference organizer. Pinchot and Sargent had developed a mutual dislike during their service together on the National Forestry Commission in 1896. Pinchot's relationship with Muir, already stretched thin by their diverging views on forest management, was at the breaking point, if not already broken, by the Hetch Hetchy controversy. With the exclusion of Muir and Sargent and others of like mind, the preservationist position had no voice at the meetings, either at the lectern or in the audience.

The conference's stated purpose of commemorating the Roosevelt administration's protection of the environment left attendees with the impression that the president subscribed to the Pinchot camp's philosophy. The "conservationist" view espoused managing natural resources on public land to provide the greatest good for the greatest number of people for the longest time. Scenic beauty, environmental integrity, or other intrinsic values merited only secondary consideration. Yet during his final address to Congress in December 1908, Roosevelt preached the contrasting "preservationist" ideal of protecting the wilderness for its own sake. He mentioned Yellowstone and Yosemite specifically, and said that, "In both, all wild things should be protected and the scenery kept wholly unmarred."

When the administration of Roosevelt's successor, William Howard Taft, inherited the Hetch Hetchy controversy upon taking office in 1909, most expected that Taft would continue the policies and programs of his predecessor. Instead, he replaced practically the entire Roosevelt cabinet with men of his own choosing. Nor was he willing to accept the outgoing interior secretary's recommendation on the Tuolumne dam as the final word. He wanted a closer look at the disputed area and arranged a trip to Yosemite with, as Roosevelt had done, Muir to lead him. They set out from San Francisco on October 6, 1909, more than forty-one years after the guide's first trip to the Valley. Taft's choice in a traveling companion understandably upset supporters of the dam. "I suppose you know, Mr. Muir," the president said, "that several people in San Francisco are very much worried because I asked you to come here with me today."

Unlike his predecessor, Taft was not an outdoorsman and the tour lasted only a day. Like Roosevelt, however, he enjoyed pelting his host with good-natured barbs. "Now that," he said of a gap where the Merced River rushed out of Yosemite Valley, "would be a fine place for a dam!"

"The man who would dam that would be damning himself!" Muir parried, much to Taft's amusement.

In more serious conversations, the president was shown maps and plans for the park, and heard arguments against damming Hetch Hetchy. He found the mountaineer's position persuasive, and told Muir he was opposed to the dam. While his itinerary did not include the dam site, Taft sent the secretary of the interior, the director of the United States Geological Survey, and a pair of government engineers off with his guide on a hasty inspection of Hetch Hetchy to see what would be lost if the proposed reservoir were built. The government party was impressed with the gorge, and left the place unwilling to inundate it. As a result of the group's report, Taft appointed a board of engineers to again study the issue, and ordered new hearings specifically to determine if San Francisco could obtain sufficient water from Lake Eleanor and leave Hetch Hetchy untouched. While no decisive action resulted, the dam was effectively halted for the remainder of his administration, giving opponents of the project time to regroup their forces for the next battle.

But the old warrior Muir grew weary of the fight. He was routinely demonized by opponents, labeled a fanatic, and portrayed as a coldhearted crusader who cared too much for nature and too little for humans. Before a congressional committee, James Phelan testified that Muir "would sacrifice his own family for the preservation of beauty." While disheartened by the attacks of his enemies, the defection of longtime supporters demoralized him. The polarizing Hetch Hetchy controversy tested loyalties and many with preservationist leanings, including some members of the Sierra Club, felt obligated to cast their lots with San Francisco and against the river valley in the mountains for which the club was named.

As president of the Sierra Club, Muir used the name and resources of the organization in presenting his arguments and petitions to government and public audiences alike. Club directors supported him and actively participated in the campaign. Some members, however, including Warren Olney, one of the founders of the organization, disapproved of the club's opposition to the dam and actively lobbied members to withdraw support for Muir and abandon the Hetch Hetchy fight. This so angered Muir that he considered resigning, both as president and as a member of the club. Others convinced him to stay, and the Hetch Hetchy question was put to a vote. By a margin of more than three to one, the members opposed the dam. Some on the losing side resigned. So embittered was founder Olney, who favored the project, that he forbade mention of Hetch Hetchy in his home forever after. Resistance from within the Sierra Club, however, ended.

Congress, meanwhile, asked the City of San Francisco to show why the needed water could not be acquired from Lake Eleanor or other sources. The city requested more time, hoping to wait out Taft and take their chances with a future administration. San Francisco was granted the first of many extensions, delaying any decision for the remainder of 1909 and through 1912.

While the Sierra Club campaign to save Hetch Hetchy continued during the delays, the battle-weary Muir, in his seventy-fourth year, took advantage of the comparatively calm period to explore the Amazon and Africa in search of new adventures and unusual trees. He could not have known that the fight for Hetch Hetchy was about to take a sinister new turn.

The aged explorer returned from his overseas adventure in March 1912, and rejoined the argument with renewed vigor. He accused the would-be dam builders of "a perfect contempt for nature." He wrote, "Dam Hetch Hetchy! As well dam for water tanks the people's cathedrals and churches, for no holier temple has ever been consecrated by the heart of man."

Then, the issue of electricity entered the Tuolumne damming debate. Opponents of the dam became convinced that water was no longer San Francisco's priority; that the city had its eye on the profits to be made from the hydroelectric potential of Hetch Hetchy. Alternative sites, which offered limited potential for power generation, had been abandoned. In 1912, lawmakers in Washington countered with an amendment to the Hetch Hetchy bill then before them. The modification eliminated any profit motive by forbidding San Francisco to sell or distribute electricity through commercial power providers, and distribute it, instead, directly to the city. Still, there was no vote on the bill and the dam question remained unanswered.

Widespread public support to save Hetch Hetchy made Muir hopeful. He wrote in his journal of the fallacy of "improving" the beauty of Yosemite National Park by burying one of its most stunning places under hundreds of feet of water. "After this is done," he scoffed, "we are promised a road blasted on the slope of the north wall, where nature lovers may sit on rustic stools, or rocks, like frogs on logs, to admire the sham dam lake, the grave of Hetch Hetchy." He voiced his long-held belief that the American people would not sit still for such desecration, and claimed "The people are now aroused. Tidings from far and near show that almost every good man and woman is with us." The entry ended on a hopeful and encouraging note: "Therefore be of good cheer, watch, and pray and fight!"

Despite public opinion now opposing the dam, his optimism proved to be short-lived. Woodrow Wilson took office as president on March 4, 1913, spelling doom for the Hetch Hetchy Valley. Wilson's choice for secretary of the interior, Franklin K. Lane, had served as city attorney of San Francisco during the administration of James Phelan.

Muir continued to fight in the face of odds even his most loyal supporters considered insurmountable. The artist William Keith, among his closest friends, feared Muir had gone over the edge in his attacks on the dam's proponents. California Congressman William Kent, who had personally donated a redwood grove on the coast north of San Francisco for a national monument named Muir Woods, believed the explorer-naturalist had become too extreme. Even Robert Underwood Johnson, an ally who had edited and published much of Muir's finest writing on wilderness preservation, deemed the cause lost and urged his friend to let it pass.

The old man felt alone and abandoned and weary of the fight. "I'll be relieved when this is settled, for it's killing me," he said in a letter to a daughter.

On December 19, 1913, President Wilson signed into law a bill allowing the City of San Francisco to dam the Tuolumne River in Yosemite National Park and turn the Hetch Hetchy Valley into a reservoir, the bottom of which, Muir predicted, would become a "drift of waste, death, and decay."

A year and five days later he, too, would be dead.

Further Earth-Planet Travels

After marriage and the birth of his first child, Muir had determined to limit his travels, put down roots, and make a success of raising grapes, pears, cherries, and a family. So, on March 25, 1881, when the captain of the revenue cutter *Thomas Corwin* invited him on a search-and-rescue expedition to the Arctic, he declined.

Lost somewhere in the frozen ocean was an exploring ship, *Jeanette,* which had been missing for two years, as well as two lost whalers. The captain of the rescue mission persisted, even enlisting Louie in the cause, and Muir was with the *Corwin* when it departed from San Francisco on May 4, 1881. By the time the ship reached the Aleutian Islands nearly two weeks later, he already had a handful of letters to post, several to his wife, some of which were to be forwarded for publication in the *San Francisco Daily Evening Bulletin,* for which he acted as correspondent, and one to his mother describing the expedition's itinerary. The ship stopped at many of the inhabited islands, questioning Aleut natives for clues about the missing ships and trading for cold-weather gear. Muir's coat, one that protected him through many a Sierra winter, proved inadequate for the Arctic, and he bartered for a fur robe.

While the *Corwin* steamed to Siberia to put ashore an exploring party that would drive dogsleds northward along the coast to search for signs of the lost ships, drifting ice shattered the cutter's rudder shaft. Makeshift repairs got them close enough for the dogsleds to reach shore across pack ice. The search party, supplied with provisions for two months and with plans for a rendezvous with the ship at Tapkan, a native village on the Siberian coast, set out with their snarling dogs and native Chukchi guides.

The *Corwin* then limped into a protected bay where the Russian navy had stockpiled coal and cleared a dry dock of sorts by blasting, chopping, and sawing away ice. The crew loaded the forward deck with borrowed coal until the ship unbalanced and the aft end tipped high enough into the air to allow proper repairs to the rudder and shaft.

Muir, meantime, studied the geography roundabout and found evidence of past glaciers, as well as delicate flowers tucked among hillside rocks to survive the harsh environment.

Once repaired, the *Corwin* steamed back across the Bering Sea to American shores and reprovisioned for the rendezvous with the Siberian search party. The ship braved fog and storms and rough seas, then found the appointed bay blocked by a three-mile barrier of shifting ice, requiring a heroic effort with the ship's boat and a fragile skin-covered craft to rescue the dogsled parties. Once safely aboard, the searchers reported that natives had found the wreck of one of the lost whalers, but they discovered no news of the other missing ships.

The cutter continued searching among the islands and along mainland shores. At one native village they found every resident dead from illegally traded alcohol, either directly from the alcohol or its aftereffects, for in their drunken stupor the villagers had failed to lay in winter supplies and starved. Muir wrote that he watched sailors gather skulls much as he had once gathered pumpkins on his family's Wisconsin farms.

He also noted that in some villages the ship visited, native hunters had wastefully exterminated entire caribou herds with newly obtained repeating rifles. Other natives, however, impressed him with their ability to establish homes and live well in such unforgiving surroundings. He found them "better behaved than white men," and "not half so greedy, shameless, or dishonest."

During the July climax of the brief Arctic summer, the scientific observer found some fifty varieties of flowers growing in valleys between slate hills, the tundra abloom, and nesting waterfowl, shore birds, and songbirds in abundance. Still, no sign of the lost ships.

Based on the last correspondence received from the lost *Jeanette*, which outlined its planned route, the rescue ship set out for "Wrangell Land." Not to be confused with Wrangell Island off Alaska's southern panhandle, this nearly mythical place off Siberia's Arctic coast, according to tradition, stretched across the North Pole and on to Greenland. Boiler iron was hung about the ship's bow and on July 30, the *Corwin* attacked the pack ice, intending, en route to Wrangell Land, to explore the six-mile-long Herald Island for signs of the lost ships.

They found no evidence of the *Jeanette,* but Muir made the most of the effort. After hacking his way up a one-hundred-foot bank of sheer ice, he found evidence of glacial action and collected specimens of fifteen plant varieties.

Dangerous fog and drifting ice slowed the ship's progress as it moved northward toward Wrangell Land. Exploring one lead after another as they temporarily opened in the ice, the captain and crew were tantalized by the sight of Wrangell's blue hills in the near distance.

Finally, in mid-August, the ship butted and caromed through five miles of block ice and reached a gravel bar at the mouth of a river. As the crew explored upstream for signs of life, Muir collected plants and located twenty species. They found no evidence of lost ships or of any other human visitation, and believed themselves the first people to set foot there. "A land more severely solitary," Muir wrote, "could hardly be found anywhere on the face of the globe." After planting an American flag, the explorers left the place in a race against the closing pack ice, and in two weeks anchored at Point Barrow on Alaska's northern shore.

The *Corwin* soon sailed north again in search of the still-missing *Jeanette,* only to be frustrated a second time by Arctic ice. They regained sight of Wrangell Land, but could not approach it, although their attempts convinced the *Corwin*'s officers that it was not the huge land of legend, merely a large island.

When the ship's ice-ramming iron sheath broke apart and a rudder chain snapped, the captain declared the expedition at an end, and on September 2, 1881, set a course for San Francisco.

Muir would later learn that the object of their search, the *Jeanette,* had been frozen in pack ice and had drifted around the Arctic Circle north and west toward Sweden, and was finally crushed and sank on June 10, 1881. Thirty-three men abandoned the ship and set out across the ice on a desperate five-hundred-mile hike to Siberia. Thirteen made it to a remote village, eleven of them survived to tell the tale. The fate of the second whaling ship remained unknown. Meanwhile, the *San Francisco Daily Evening Bulletin* had published much of the correspondence Muir had sent home. (It was collected after his death in book form as *The Cruise of the Corwin.*)

The author's self-imposed exile from travel took hold in earnest when he returned to his orchards and vineyards in Martinez, and he devoted his attention almost fully to improving production and profitability. The physical toll was heavy, however, and confinement in the hot, low country caused a persistent cough, loss of appetite, irritability, and depression. By 1888, he had had about all he could stand of the settled life. Louie's concern for his health heightened, too, and, based on the quality of his contributions as a writer and editor of the book *Picturesque California,* she also feared his work as a grower had taken a toll on his literary potential.

Completion of *Picturesque California* required a trip to the Northwest, so he invited a friend, the artist William Keith, along for some wilderness adventure. They set out in early July 1888, stopping over at Mount Shasta, one of the mountaineer's favorite haunts, then proceeded to Portland, where they hoped to scale Mount Hood. Keith had taken ill, however, so they moved on to Seattle, determined to climb to the 14,410-foot summit of Mount Rainier.

"The people about the towns and mills and mines and rail-roads are fairly drunk with the joy of material action and achievement," Muir wrote of the Seattle vicinity. "Just hear the hiss of steel saws making boards enough for a house every minute of the night and day, and the ring of the axe in the woods. The chips are flying in a perpetual storm, thick as flakes of snow." He also saw a quieter, more serene side of the area. "A calm morning. The [Puget] Sound silvery smooth of spangles. Detail of mountain sculpture lost in a fine fading-edged haze of white. The summit of Mount Rainier clear . . . with glaciers glistening."

They set out for the mountain on August 8, "A fine sunny day, with glorious views of Rainier," according to a journal entry. Heavily laden "Washington mules and cayuses" packed the party and their provisions up the forested slopes with a young guide who "knew the mysterious diamond hitch," a complex but effective method of lashing loads to pack animals.

Muir enjoyed leaving camp at night for solitary walks in the woods, and wrote that "the stillness is at once awful and sublime. Every leaf seems to speak. One gets close to Nature, and the love of beauty grows as it cannot in the distractions of a camp."

He wrote that when scaling treacherous slopes by daylight, however, beauty took a backseat. "In climbing where the danger is great, all attention has to be given the ground step by step, leaving nothing for beauty by the way." The intense concentration had its reward, making one feel so alive, he said, that by comparison ordinary existence was akin to sleep. Senses heightened by hazards made the payoff well worth the effort required to earn it. "On the summit with the grand outlook—all the world spread out below—one is able to see it better," he wrote, "and reaps richer harvests than would have been possible ere the presence of danger summoned him to life." The Rainier journal entries close with a curious caution: "But woe to the climber, however ambitious, who has had the misfortune to indulge in tobacco and beer. He is easily nerve-shaken and daunted."

The life-changing letter from Louie, voicing her concern that ranch work exacted too great a toll on his health and distracted him from his true calling, found Muir in Seattle after the climb. At her insistence, he rid himself of day-to-day horticultural responsibilities and with the burden lifted, his literary ambitions again bore fruit and his wanderlust blossomed.

"On the fourteenth of June, 1890, I set forth from San Francisco on my fourth excursion to the grand wilderness of Alaska, full of eager, faithful hope, for every excursion that I have made in all my rambling life has been fruitful and delightful," he wrote of his next major ramble. "All the wild world is beautiful, and it matters but little where we go . . . everywhere and always we are in God's eternal beauty and love."

He returned to studies interrupted a decade earlier, charting the glaciers feeding into Glacier Bay. "I had visited them in a canoe twice before this," he recorded in his journal, "But I had seen but little of their sources, and I was eager to make my way back into the mountains where their countless tributaries take their rise." He also hoped to measure the speed of the glaciers' movement and count the icebergs they discharged into the bay.

Muir seldom allowed scientific pursuits to interfere with his reveling in the wonders of nature, and this journey was no different. "In the early afternoon a dense haze fills the sky," he wrote of the late June days at Glacier Bay. "The sun seen through this becomes a globe of glorious ruby, and its glare on the sea looks as if the water had been strewn with a crystalline ruby-dust."

He set out alone on July 11, upstream along the largest river of ice, Muir Glacier. "I am often asked if I am not lonesome on my solitary excursions," he wrote. "It seems so self-evident that one cannot be lonesome where everything is wild and beautiful and busy and steeped with God that the question is hard to answer—seems silly."

Even for Muir, however, solitary travel had its dangers. Four days later, on July 15, he climbed to the top of a three-thousand-foot mountain to study the lay of the land, then attempted to ride back down on the handmade sled that held his provisions. He lost control on the ice and tumbled down the slope, stopping only upon reaching an expanse of loose talus. Unhurt but stunned, he watched ravens circling overhead. "Not yet, you black imps, not yet," he said. "Wait awhile, I'm not carrion yet."

The next day and night were spent cold and wet on the bare expanse of the glacier, burning wood shavings from the bottom of his sled in a tin cup to heat ice melt in a second cup for tea. Two days later, the relentless glare of Arctic sun off glacier ice had him seeing double, and the next day he had nearly gone blind. Determination and a makeshift pair of goggles got him to the glacier's edge, where he gathered firewood then rejuvenated and fortified himself with enough hot tea to fuel his return to the bay.

He pressed on the following day, July 20, and late in the

afternoon stepped into an invisible water-filled crevasse, soaking himself thoroughly. He laboriously clawed out of the icy bath, found shelter from the wind, and stripped off wet clothes for a long, cold night in a sleeping bag. His eleven-day journey in a pristine wilderness, a place probably unseen by any other white man, ended when he reached Muir Inlet on Glacier Bay the next afternoon and met up with companions waiting there.

His journal entries from the trip say little about the hazards, and much about the wonders:

In God's wilderness lies the hope of the world.

Ice sheet brooding with supreme dominion over the coming landscape, clasping a thousand mountains in its crystal embrace.

A multitude of mountains glowing in bright and lovely color like any flower.

Sleeping by a waterfall in a lonely canyon is impressive, but more so sleeping by a waterfall on a great glacier far from land.

In this silent, serene wilderness the weary can gain a heart-bath in perfect peace.

At night, such a chaste icy freshness came down the glacier on the sweet north wind.

By early September he had returned home to Martinez, his physical and emotional health improved despite the dangers and mishaps of his fourth Alaska expedition. He revisited several favorite sites in the Sierra during 1892, helped found the

Sierra Club, traveled to Wisconsin in a failed effort to rescue a brother-in-law's business, and became heavily involved in a campaign to defeat legislation to reduce the size of Yosemite National Park.

By 1893, he was again ready to travel. He and artist companion William Keith had long contemplated a trip to Europe together, and when a letter from his friend arrived in June saying the time was right, Muir jumped at the chance. They arranged to meet in Chicago, where the World's Columbian Exposition was under way, but Keith had tired of the crowds by the time Muir arrived and left word to meet him in New York. In a letter to Louie, Muir wrote that the Chicago Exposition was a "rat's nest," and soon followed Keith to New York.

There, the popular California painter was caught up in a whirl of parties, gallery tours, and entertainments hosted by the art community in his behalf. Robert Underwood Johnson of *Century* magazine soon had his wilderness writer and preservationist ally busy with a similar social spin in literary circles. Muir met several writers of note, including fellow naturalist John Burroughs, Rudyard Kipling, and Mark Twain, and expressed surprise that they knew of him. "I had no idea I was so well known," he confessed in a letter to Louie, "considering how little I have written." He dined at the Pinchot mansion in Gramercy Park and talked forestry with young Gifford. Johnson also escorted his visiting celebrity to Boston, Cambridge, and Concord. At Sleepy Hollow Cemetery Muir paid his respects at the graves of men he considered among his most important influences—Nathaniel Hawthorne, Henry David Thoreau, and his friend Ralph Waldo Emerson. Johnson also took Muir to the Brookline, Massachusetts, estate of Charles Sargent, and this first meeting with the famous Harvard horticulturist grew into a lasting friendship.

When he finally managed to extricate himself from Johnson's grasp near the end of June, Muir's would-be traveling companion Keith had long since sailed for Europe and Muir followed in his wake, hoping to finally link up somewhere across the Atlantic. He landed in Liverpool in early July and left immediately for Edinburgh, toured the city, then boarded an eastbound train for his hometown of Dunbar on the shore of the North Sea.

His boyhood home was now a hotel, and from the street he studied the upper-story dormer window through which he and his younger brother David had climbed one windy night for a "good scootcher," attempting to reconcile his memory of the adventure with the reality of where it happened. He revisited the tumbled-down walls of Dunbar Castle, over which he had scaled and scrambled as an aspiring climber. He looked up childhood friends, met a cousin, visited the old school, and wandered the nearby hills. "I seemed a boy again," the fifty-five-year-old man wrote in a letter to a daughter, "and all the long years in America were forgotten."

He would return to Dunbar in September, at the end of his tour. In the interval, he visited Norway's glacial fjords, the Lake District of England, the Houses of Parliament at Westminster Palace in London, the Matterhorn in Switzerland, and the bogs and lakes of Ireland. He was back at home in Martinez in October, having never joined up with his traveling companion William Keith.

Most of the next two years were devoted to writing, with travel largely restricted to the Sierra and Southern California, but in 1896 Muir crossed and recrossed the continent from coast to coast and from the southwestern deserts to Alaska's southern shores. Travels with the National Forestry Commission determined much of his itinerary, a grand tour of forests the government had set aside but failed to manage.

While the commission made its plans, Muir made plans to travel to Cambridge, Massachusetts, where he would be given an honorary degree during Harvard's June 24, 1896, commencement exercises. He changed his route and schedule when a mystical premonition informed him that his mother lay dying. His presence at her Wisconsin home lifted her spirits and her health improved, so he proceeded eastward. The rally did not last, however. After accepting his honors at Harvard he returned to Wisconsin for her funeral, then joined the Commission in Chicago on July 5.

The trip started by train, but it would involve a riverboat, rowboat, wagons, carriages, mules, saddle horses, and shank's mare before it finished. After visiting mountain forests in the Black Hills, Bighorns, Bitterroots, and Cascades, Muir left the commission in Washington State and traveled to Tacoma. There he joined Henry Fairfield Osborn, famed paleontologist of the American Museum of Natural History and one of many new friends from Muir's 1893 visit to New York City, during which he had spent several days with the Osborn family at their plush Hudson River estate. Now the scientist and the naturalist planned to visit the bays and inlets of Prince William Sound on Alaska's southern shore. After the brief trip, Muir rejoined the Forest Commission in Oregon, meeting Charles Sargent in Ashland on August 27, and departing the same day for Crater Lake in the Cascades.

"The lake walls of thirty to ninety degrees descended to the shore, where the slope averages thirty-five degrees," he recorded in his journal on August 30. Crater Island seemed afloat in the deep blue lake, "a fine symmetrical volcano and comparatively recent." Several members of the commission boarded a small rowboat and set out for the island, despite threatening skies. "Halfway over it began to thunder and whitecaps broke into our overloaded boat," he wrote. They regained the shore, built a fire to dry their clothes, then rowed along the lakeshore to the trailhead below their campsite and "climbed up to camp; rather tired but none the worse—rather better for the exercise."

The commission headed southwest to Grant's Pass, the Pacific coast, and Crescent City, California. "Examined the mill, and went out on a logging train a few miles and saw the work of ruin going on," Muir said. "It takes three-quarters of a day for two men to down a tree eight feet in diameter." Following the Coast Ranges' redwood belt south as far as Ukiah, California, the commissioners boarded a train there for San Francisco. On September 10, Muir wrote that he "Went home on the nine o'clock train. Saw my wife and babies, changed clothing, repacked satchel ready to rejoin party next day." The commission stayed in California until late September, touring more of the Coast Ranges, the Sierra Nevada, and the San Bernardino and San Jacinto Mountains of Southern California.

"Set out from Flagstaff [Arizona] for the Grand Canyon," he recorded on September 28. "I ran up to the verge of the canyon and had my first memorable and overwhelming view in the light and shade of the setting sun," he said of his initial encounter with the gorge. He continued the description in a poetic vein: ". . . turrets, towers, pyramids, battlemented castles, rising in glowing beauty from the depths of this canyon of canyons noiselessly hewn from the smooth mass of this featureless plateau." Muir and Gifford Pinchot spent many hours together hiking the canyon rim, fascinated with its "endless changing views" and colors. "Reds, grays, ashy greens of varied limestones and sandstones, lavender, and tones nameless and numberless."

Some members of the commission returned to Flagstaff on September 30. Muir, however, said that he and a few others "went to the bottom of the canyon down the Hance Trail." Even in the midst of the incomparable geology of Grand Canyon, his love for botany surfaced. "Much Clematis on the way," he wrote, "and charming Abronia near the foot of the trail." He left the canyon the next day, ending his travels with the commission, and returned to Martinez and his family while the commissioners traveled through the forest reserves of Colorado on their return east.

In 1897, Alaska beckoned for the sixth time. He accompanied Charles Sargent and the botanist William Canby in August to the southeastern Alaskan panhandle to study the forests there, as well as the woods of western Canada. They stopped in Seattle on the way home, and there the legendary meeting with Gifford Pinchot in a hotel lobby is said to have marked the end of a friendship and the beginning of a serious rift in the environmental movement—all because of a purported, mutually intolerable, disagreement over sheep.

He took to the trail, again with Sargent as a traveling companion, in the fall of 1898. In a September 8 journal entry, Muir reported that he "Spent the day at Sargent's, sleeping, sauntering, reading." Five days later they were in the Appalachian Mountains in the North Carolina–Tennessee border country near Johnson City, Tennessee, "High on Roan Bluff, over sixty-two hundred feet above sea-level," he wrote. "We came up here by surrey from Cranberry, eighteen miles, through a glorious mountain forest." The travel by surrey represented a marked difference from his thousand-mile hike through the region in 1867.

The mountaineer jumped about in joy, reveling in the flaming fall colors, and teased his staid New England companion. "There you stand in the face of all heaven come down to earth," he said, "like a critic of the universe, as if to say, 'Come, Nature, bring on the best you have. I'm from BOSTON!'"

They intended to travel to Florida, but Sargent took ill and returned home, interrupting their trip until November. Muir used the disruption to visit his editor friend Robert Underwood Johnson in New York City, spend time with Henry Fairfield Osborn and his family at "Wing-and-Wing," their estate on the Hudson River, and visit other people and places in New York and New England. On November 8, he met Sargent and William Canby in Wilmington, Delaware, and they set out once more on their delayed journey to Florida.

By November 11, they reached St. Augustine, moved on to Miami, then to the extreme of the continent at Key West, "a miserable place of squalid shanties," according to a journal entry. The botanists were impressed, however, with the flora. "Saw a wonderful Ficus, or banyan tree, with ten feet or more of compound trunk from descending root, bracing, reinforcing the most complicated trunk imaginable, with leaves a shiny bright green and thrifty looking," he wrote. "No wind can overthrow such a tree."

They traveled next to Cedar Keys, off the peninsula's west coast, where Muir had been stricken with malaria on his 1867 visit. He learned that the sawmill operator who employed him briefly had died, but that the man's wife, who had nursed the sick worker, was living in a nearby inland town called Archer. She did not recognize her former patient, but was excited to learn his name when the visitor introduced himself. "'The California John Muir?' she almost screamed," he reported. "Then," he said, "she introduced me to her friends, telling them that thirty-odd years ago I was the finest, handsomest young man one could hope to see, etc." She had not forgotten him, knew of his explorations and writing, and, he said, "knew the Muir Glacier must have been named for me." The travelers parted ways there November 22, Sargent and Canby going north and Muir west, returning home to California via Mobile, New Orleans, and Texas.

In 1899, Alaska called yet again, this time with the voice of railroad millionaire Edward H. Harriman. The magnate's doctor had prescribed an extended vacation to ward off exhaustion and, wanting to combine public service with his pleasure, the industrialist concocted a remarkable outing. He would charter a steamer, make provisions on board for his family, then outfit the remainder of the ship to accommodate as many scientists, naturalists, and artists as it would hold—which turned out to be about twenty-five, Muir among them.

Muir almost declined Harriman's invitation. He believed,

like many of his day, that railroaders and industrialists had despoiled and destroyed too much of nature in their reckless pursuit of profit. The lure of the destination, however— Alaska—proved too strong and he steamed out of Portland, Oregon with the expedition on May 31. His host initially "repelled" him but he eventually "learned to love him," even if, for a time, he remained dubious of his host's motives. When fellow scientists were singing the magnate's praises and extolling the benefits of his wealth, Muir countered, "I don't think Mr. Harriman is very rich. He has not as much money as I have. I have all I want and Mr. Harriman has not." There were no secrets aboard ship, and word soon reached the millionaire, who answered his critic. "I never cared for money except as power for work," he said, ". . . in doing good, helping to feed man and beast, and making everybody and everything a little better."

Throughout the journey, Muir kept a running account of the trees, flowers, and shrubs he observed every time the ship put ashore, which was often, along with notes on birds, animals, mountains, and, of course, glaciers. At Glacier Bay on June 9, he wrote of "A grand berg discharge." A two-hundred-foot-long mass of ice broke free and slid into the bay, then rose out of the deep "a hundred and fifty feet, the water like hair streaming from it."

The group spent five days at Glacier Bay studying the rivers of ice pouring down and littering the water with icebergs large and small. Another of the expedition's well-known naturalists, John Burroughs, remarked in jest that, "In John Muir we had an authority on glaciers, and a thorough one—so thorough that he would not allow the rest of the party to have an opinion on the subject." Indeed an authority, Muir knew the glaciers well, and could see how the landscape had changed since his earlier visits. A large glacier he had first christened the "Grand Pacific" had retreated several miles and separated into three smaller ones. In honor of his host, he named the largest of the three "Harriman Glacier" and later gave the railroader's name to a hidden fjord the expedition discovered at Prince William Sound.

The voyagers visited many other sites on the Alaskan coast, a number of islands, and even crossed the Bering Sea for a look at Siberia before returning to Seattle, where the party put ashore for the last time on July 29.

Friend and frequent traveling companion Charles Sargent convinced Muir to accompany him on another jaunt—this one a "world tour of trees," to leave from the East Coast in the spring of 1903. The Californian had to delay the departure date, however, when President Theodore Roosevelt submitted a personal request to be guided through the Yosemite region. After fulfilling that obligation, Muir and Sargent boarded a ship for Europe on a trip made much easier through the assistance of another former traveling companion, Edward H. Harriman, who provided the tourists free passage on his steamship lines, and whose staff assisted with travel arrangements.

Still, it was not an easy journey for Muir, who, at sixty-five, lacked the vigor he enjoyed in his rambling youth. Poor health and illness dogged him throughout Europe, to the point that he had to be loaded on a train on a stretcher for one leg of the journey. His spirits would rally temporarily when in the woods or rural areas, but he soon tired of visiting cities. He expressed pleasure when their party boarded a train in early August for a long ride across wide-open Siberia and Manchuria. Once in

Manchuria, however, ptomaine poisoning struck him, and the visit and his senses were dulled by morphine and brandy.

Tired, weak, emaciated, and ill, he decided to leave Sargent at Shanghai, and strike out on his own for the Himalayas. He sensed that the mountains, along with the reduced stress of solo travel, would be rejuvenating. Besides, the Himalayas, as with any mountains, proved an irresistible lure, and he longed to see a variety of cedar tree, the deodar, that grew there. He would see both the mountains and the trees at Simla, a northern Indian town and summer capital, although his still-fragile health would not allow any attempt at climbing. He went on to visit the pyramids and Suez Canal of Egypt, the unfamiliar and therefore exciting flora of Australia and New Zealand, and, finally, enjoyed a long voyage home being pampered on a Harriman ship. He walked down the gangplank in San Francisco on May 27, 1904, feeling fit despite the rigors of a year abroad.

Muir stayed close to home for most of the next year, lobbying politicians to remove Yosemite Valley from the grasp of the State of California and include it in the surrounding national park. His next journey of note began in May 1905, but neither the trip nor the destination were of his choosing. His wife, Louie, was ill, but their daughter Helen Lillian's health was even poorer as she seemed unable to shake the effects of her latest of many bouts with pneumonia. Doctors recommended a drier climate, so the concerned father saw no choice but to set out with his ailing daughter for the deserts of southeastern Arizona, accompanied by his older daughter, Annie Wanda. They settled into an open-air camp on Rancho Bonita, an expansive "twenty-by-thirty-mile ranch, with its famous flocks and herds," owned by "Don Pedro," who, Muir said in his notebooks, was "one of the noblest, most devoutly revered enrichments of my life."

Melancholy, probably a result of worry over his family's health, showed in Muir's journal entries. "Radiant days and months, hot, dry, with a tinge of sadness and haze on the horizon," he wrote of the desert, and, "A great calm day fading like a flower purple in the morning, and glowing noon, purple and crimson in the evening—fading like a flower."

The people he met lifted his spirits. "There are no shallow, colorless people in Arizona," he wrote. "Like the rings of wood in trees, the wonder-working climate has been absorbed in rings of character." Even the workingmen merited his admiration. "The cowboys on horseback are superbly statuesque without an apparent desire to pose."

The healing air earned his highest praise, however. "I never breathed air more distinctly, palpably good," he wrote. "It fairly thrills and quivers, as if one actually felt the beatings of the infinitely small vital electric waves of life and light drenching every cell of flesh and bone, bringing on a complete resurrection after the death of sound sleep."

An urgent cable from Martinez sent Muir back home, where he found Louie in a hopeless condition from advanced lung cancer. After her burial in the family cemetery he returned to Arizona mourning the loss of a remarkable companion. This time, father and daughters set up housekeeping at a tourist hotel, with Helen Lillian in a tent outside, near the Petrified Forest, just east of Holbrook in the northeastern quarter of the territory. Sometimes alone, sometimes with his girls, the grieving widower wandered through a forest much different from any other of his long experience: hardened by absorbing silica from water over the ages, huge tree trunks turned to stone lay scattered across the dry sand.

Tourists collecting the fossil trees for souvenirs troubled him, and commercial interests—primarily the Santa Fe Railroad— bothered him even more, as they broke the stone trunks to bits and polished them into salable baubles. Early in 1906, Congress passed the Antiquities Act, which allowed the president to arbitrarily set aside areas whose scenic, scientific, or historic interest merited protection. Muir convinced his friend in the White House, Theodore Roosevelt, to use this new power to declare the Petrified Forest a national monument. It was later expanded and made a national park.

In mid-1906 Muir returned to Martinez, his daughter Annie Wanda now married and living in her late grandfather Strentzel's old house, and a fully recovered Helen Lillian living with her father in the main ranch house.

For several years to come he limited his travels and fought to prevent the damming of Hetch Hetchy Valley in Yosemite National Park. He found time to journey to Harriman's Pelican Bay Lodge near Klamath Falls, Oregon, for an extended stay and some writing time in the summer of 1907. In February 1909, he met John Burroughs at the Petrified Forest and toured with him there and at the Grand Canyon.

A brief but remarkable excursion interrupted his travels with Burroughs, and again, Harriman was involved. Muir rode in the millionaire's private railroad car to the Salton Sea in southwestern California's Imperial Valley; the "sea" the result of a breakout of the Colorado River, which poured tons and acres of water into a desert basin. After the federal government despaired of stemming the flow, Harriman had filled the breach with trainload after trainload of boulders. Now, he wanted his friend's expert opinion as a geologist on the prospects of future flood control. Following the interruption, Muir rejoined Burroughs in California in May and guided his party through Yosemite.

In 1867, when he had determined to become a "tramp" and set out walking through the Southern states to the Gulf of Mexico, his plan had been to continue southward and explore the Amazon Basin of South America, in imitation of the great German naturalist Alexander von Humboldt. In 1911, at age seventy-four and against the advice of virtually everyone he knew, he set out alone to finally realize the dream. He reached the Amazon on August 31 and continued upriver by steamboat for a thousand miles, paying close attention to the luxuriant foliage all the while. His hope of locating a rare water lily on the Amazon and its Rio Negro tributary went unfulfilled. Another search, for the monkey puzzle tree, or Chile pine, was finally rewarded and he spent a night sleeping among them high in the Andes.

His desire to see another rare tree, the baobab, took him across the South Atlantic to South Africa. He reached Cape Town in January 1912, and took a train to Victoria Falls. After baffling a hotel manager with his request to direct him to a specimen of the tree, a boy on the street took him to a grove near the falls. The object of his curiosity rivaled the sequoia in girth. (While no taller than a common maple, the massive baobab's trunk can reach thirty feet in diameter.)

After this excursion, he took a ship up the east coast of the continent and journeyed inland to the headwaters of the Nile

River before returning to America via the Mediterranean and the Atlantic. He ended his adventure in New York City on March 26, 1912, seven months after departing.

Muir's next big journey would wait for more than two and a half years. While he did not look forward to the trip, he did not fear it. "The rugged old Norsemen," he said, "wrote of death as *Heimgang*—home-going."

The Writing Life

Muir's approach to the craft of writing can be likened to the Creator's approach to making mammals. A set of bones used to build a flipper for a whale can be refashioned to make a wing for a bat, then modified again to make a hand for a human. Likewise, our writer's journal entries found their way into letters, which became newspaper stories, were later fashioned into magazine articles, then gathered as essay collections or included in the narrative of books.

This economy of words—economical only in the sense of recycling, as the naturalist's style could be both florid and verbose—may have been due to his dislike of the writing process. He did not enjoy the work, finding it difficult and tedious, nor was he satisfied with the result of his effort, finding prose a weak instrument for the reality he wished to convey. Had he not been urged by friends, most notably Jeanne Carr, to take up the pen initially, and had he not been continually prodded by her, his wife, and his editors to keep writing, it is unlikely the skeptical Muir would have left the wealth of words he did. "No amount of word-making will ever make a single soul to *know* these mountains," he wrote in 1872. "One day's exposure to mountains is better than a cartload of books."

While he did not leave a cartload of books, six volumes of his writing were published while he lived, four others posthumously. Adding to the count are several other books, created by clipping Muir's essays and articles from various published sources and pasting them together in new, thematic collections. More important than the quantity of his writing, however, is the quality, in the sense of its lasting effect on American culture in helping to create the desire and will to protect and preserve wild and natural environments.

His first appearance in print was inadvertent. While traveling in Canada in 1864, a long day of splashing through chilly marshes led to the discovery of a rare flower, *Calypso borealis,* the "hider of the north." The find was reported in an 1866 letter to Jeanne Carr, which was copied—without her knowledge or permission—by a visitor to her home who then submitted it to the *Boston Recorder* as part of a letter of his own. Carr's visitor did not claim authorship of the borrowed words, but neither did he name the author, referring to him only as "a young Wisconsin gatherer of simples" and an "inspired pilgrim." Carr was peeved. "There is no law against such an indelicate and outrageous abuse of the privileges of friendship. Except the law of one's mind—but his punishment shall be that he never lays finger on letter of mine again," she wrote to Muir, informing him of the incident.

Even upon taking up pen and notebook in a purposeful way

in 1867, at age twenty-nine, to record his travels, it is unlikely that thoughts of publication were among the wanderer's reasons for doing so. While he remained a prolific letter writer and journal keeper, fluently dashing off accounts of his discoveries, thoughts, and ideas, when he took up writing for publication he became slow and meticulous, editing and rewriting endlessly until the process became tiresome and painful. He wondered if it was worth the effort. "It seems strange," he recorded in his journal upon completing a magazine article, "that a paper that reads smoothly and may be finished in ten minutes should require months to write."

Interest in the scientific community about his theories of glacial action in the Yosemite finally stirred his desire to write, and he determined to see his ideas in print no matter the difficulty. He had circulated his conclusions informally, sharing them in letters to friends and scientists, and he had personally guided anyone with an interest in geology to sites in the valley and the Sierra above that displayed evidence supporting his theories. These visitors and correspondents encouraged him to publish his findings and give them the exposure they deserved. "Some of my friends are badgering me to write for some of the magazines, and I am almost tempted to try it," he told Jeanne Carr in a September 1871 letter, "only I am afraid that this would distract my mind from my work more than the distasteful and depressing labor of the mill or of guiding. What do you think about it?"

She was all for it. In fact, one of the friends urging him to write, the Smithsonian Institution's Dr. Clinton L. Merriam, had visited the mountaineer at Yosemite through an introduction from Carr. The reluctant writer finally prepared a report on Sierra glaciers, and with assistance from the influential Dr. Merriam, the article appeared in the December 8, 1871, issue of the *New York Daily Tribune*. The paper paid two hundred dollars for the story, Muir's first money as a writer.

Shortly after the glacier story appeared in the Eastern newspaper, Muir sent Carr a report of a glorious but severe winter snow and rainstorm. "I have tried to put it in form for publication, and if you can rasp off the rougher angles and wedge in a few slippery words between bad splices perhaps it may be sufficiently civilized for *Overland* or *Atlantic*," he wrote, referring to two of the day's popular literary magazines, one published in the West, the other in the East. He was not hopeful about the prospects of what he judged weak prose. "I confide my dead friend to your keeping, and you may print what you like," he told her of the story he titled "Jubilee of the Waters."

In January 1872, his mentor submitted the story to the magazine founded by Bret Harte, *The Overland Monthly*, with a short letter saying the writer was "as modest as he is gifted, and utterly devoid of literary ambition," and she offered the paper on her "own responsibility." The story appeared in the April issue under the title "Yosemite Valley in Flood."

As Muir continued to publish in the *New York Daily Tribune*, and with the acceptance of more stories by *The Overland Monthly*, he grew to believe that writing might provide an income in addition to creating appreciation for the wonders of nature. Carr lent valuable assistance along the way, including editing and rewriting, even calling on her famous friend Ralph Waldo Emerson for help in persuading the editor of *The Atlantic Monthly* to publish her protégé. "You are not to know anything about it," she said in a letter to Muir about the submission. "Let it take its chances." She would submit many of his pieces to other periodicals under similar circumstances, often without his knowledge but always with his total trust.

Even his success at publication did little to inspire confidence in the writer. "The few hard words make but a skeleton, fleshless, heartless, and when you read, the dead, bony words rattle in one's teeth," he confided to Carr in a March 1873 letter. His disappointment did not discourage effort, however. "Yet I will not the less endeavor to do my poor best, believing that even these dead bone heaps called articles will occasionally contain hints to some living souls who know how to find them."

While seemingly humble about his talent as a writer, Muir was confident in his interpretation of the evidence showing that the primary shaper of the splendidly distinctive Yosemite Valley had been glacial action from the Sierra above. In 1871, in some detail, he had told Carr in a letter about "the only book I ever invented," a book that would explain how "each dome and brow and wall and every grace and spire and brother is the necessary result of the delicately balanced blows of well-directed and combined glaciers." The time arrived, in 1873, for him to finally put his ideas on paper in comprehensive detail and submit his theories for a public airing. It would not be in book form, however. He decided to write a sequence of articles for *The Overland Monthly* magazine for publication under the title "Studies in the Sierra."

He left Yosemite in November, determined to spend the winter with the Carrs and fashion the notes, sketches, and diagrams in his Sierra glacier journals into articles suitable for publication. A few weeks earlier, however, a son of the Carrs had been killed in a railroad accident, so he opted instead to stay with other friends in Oakland. For ten months he would huddle in an upstairs room for hours on end grinding out words with the relentless persistence of the ice sheets of which he wrote. The first article appeared in May 1874, with another following each month through January 1875. Although published in a literary journal, "Studies in the Sierra" aroused a good deal of interest and controversy in the scientific community and contributed to the feud between Muir, the amateur geologist, and Josiah Whitney, distinguished professor and head of the California State Geological Survey. Whitney denied the influence of glaciers in the creation of Yosemite, attributing the unique characteristics of the gorge to a cataclysmic subsidence of the earth's crust. In the end, Muir's theories won out and the explanation of the eminent geologist was discredited and discarded.

Being cooped up in the city, self-imprisoned in a study, hunched over a writing desk, held no appeal to a born roamer, but visits to and from friends, filled with animated conversations and spirited debate, relieved the monotony. William Keith, the well-known landscape artist, was a regular. Joseph LeConte, a geology professor who had toured the Yosemite with Muir, visited frequently, along with his brother John, president of the University of California. Jeanne and Ezra Carr often invited Muir to their home.

Society was no substitute for the Sierra, however, and as soon as the writer placed the period at the end of the final sentence of "Studies in the Sierra" in September 1874, he left the city to return to Yosemite. "The freedom I felt was exhilarating," he wrote to Carr soon after his arrival. "Before I had walked ten miles, I was wearied and footsore, but it was real earnest work and I liked it. Any kind of simple, natural destruction is preferable to the numb, dumb apathetic deaths of a town." Although already a familiar face in the high country, he found a new kind of recognition. "I met many hearty, shaggy mountaineers, glad to see me," he said of his visit to the foothills town of Coulterville. "Strange to say, the *Overland* 'Studies' have been read and discussed in the most unlikely places. Some numbers have found their way through the Bloody Canyon pass to Mono," a lakeshore settlement below the eastern scarp of the Sierra.

The lengthy letter proceeded to describe other places he visited on his tour and his exultation in the natural glories he found. Something, however, was missing. "No one of the rocks seems to call me now, nor any of the distant mountains. Surely this Merced and Tuolumne chapter of my life is done," he said, referring to the two principal rivers that drain the Yosemite region. Of the valley itself, he said, "I feel that I am a stranger here. . . . I will go out in a day or so."

He wandered off toward Mount Shasta and found time along the way to write a "letter" to the *San Francisco Daily Evening Bulletin,* the first of many submissions to the paper reporting his many travels to come. His writings continued to be published in *The Overland Monthly* and his work began to appear in *Scribner's Monthly* as well. His first publication there became one of his most popular essays, a report titled "A Windstorm in the Yuba" whose climactic passage finds the observer of the December storm more than a hundred feet up a tree riding out the gale "like a bobolink on a reed."

A few months after coming down the tree, he was back at

Mount Shasta where he found inspiration for another story. With companion and guide Jerome Fay, Muir climbed the 14,142-foot mountain to chart the summit for the United States Coast and Geodetic Survey. A violent winter storm caught the pair on the exposed slopes, where they were forced to spend the night of April 30, 1875, among geothermal gas vents and fumaroles, freezing in the bitter wind and scalded by the steaming mud. The popular "A Perilous Night on Mount Shasta" was the result.

Muir returned to the Bay Area and once more found lodgings in an upper room of a friend's house, this time in San Francisco. This became his headquarters for a time, as he alternated intensive periods of writing with frequent travels far and near. Circulation of his writing increased with the addition of *Harper's New Monthly Magazine* to the list of periodicals that regularly featured his work. His name and his writings became more familiar to Eastern readers, and with the wider audience his work gradually evolved from natural history essays and accounts of adventuresome travels toward impassioned pleas for the protection of forests. His first sermon on the subject was published February 5, 1876, under the title "God's First Temples: How Shall We Preserve our Forests?" in the *Sacramento Daily Union*.

He continued to agonize over his prose, and the friends who listened to him read his work offered advice. His landlord once suggested that he "Stop revising so much. You make your style so slippery a man can't stand on it." Many an evening, the storyteller held the man's children enthralled with his tales, and one night he advised Muir to "go upstairs and write that down just as you have told it to us." The advice proved valuable, and many of the writer's most popular essays were written in that upstairs room in San Francisco. The environment remained congenial, and from 1875 through 1878, Muir would return there sporadically to write when between his many journeys. Included in these were visits to Utah's Wasatch Mountains and Southern California's San Gabriel range, a trip with Harvard botanist Asa Gray to Mount Shasta and the Rancho Chico home of California pioneer John Bidwell, and an expedition for the United States Coast and Geodetic Survey to the Great Basin in Nevada and Utah. The *San Francisco Daily Evening Bulletin* regularly published correspondence from the traveler, and these reports, along with his letters and journals, would also be reworked for magazine articles and later, books.

Muir's services as a correspondent for the San Francisco newspaper continued during his 1879 and 1880 Alaska expeditions, and the 1881 Arctic expedition aboard the *Corwin* to search for a missing exploring ship and two lost whaling vessels. No other articles or essays beyond his newspaper reports were fashioned from these adventures, however—at least for a time. He had married Louie Wanda Strentzel in 1880, and as he became more and more involved and overwhelmed with management and operation of the family orchards and vineyards, he set his journals aside and his writing, like his traveling, slowed and virtually stopped until 1889.

One exception during the decade-long interval was the book *Picturesque California*. In 1887, Muir agreed to both edit and contribute to the two-volume, oversized, colorful, illustrated advertisement for the state. In a curious reversal of roles, he persuaded Jeanne Carr to contribute a chapter on Southern

California. His October 22 letter to her said, "I told Mr. Dewing [the publisher] that I thought you could write Southern California better than anybody else that I knew, and that he better let you try your hand on an article or two." He was sketchy, however, on the terms. "As to compensation, I know very little about it," he wrote. "Go ahead and write an article and send in your bill is my advice." He went on to provide a good deal of information about his expectations for content, concluding with: "What a bright appreciative traveler would like to see and hear is what is wanted as near as I can make out."

Her progress by January, it seems, proved less than satisfactory for his letter of the twelfth said, "I saw from your first manuscript that you had difficulty getting launched. You were trying to do too much." By the end of the month, the piece had gone from bad to worse. "My knowledge of Southern California is not sufficiently close to enable me to follow you well in your descriptions and the manuscript is so mixed and disjointed that I cannot in some places find out where or in what direction you are driving," he wrote. He encouraged her to take "all the time you require to make the work satisfactory to yourself" and to expect "the company" to provide specific information about "what to omit and what to include and the relative importance of the sections, etc., etc."

Muir himself had difficulty with his own original pieces for the book and Louie, his wife and critic, found his words dull and encouraged him to do better. Most of his contributions, however, were merely reworked versions of earlier pieces on Yosemite, the Sierra, and other subjects about which he had written widely and well. The book eventually went to press, more than a year past deadline.

If *Picturesque California* got Muir back in the writing saddle, Robert Underwood Johnson supplied the spurs and quirt. Johnson was associate editor of *The Century* magazine, the successor to *Scribner's Monthly* and one of America's most popular and influential periodicals. He had worked his way up through the publishing empire of Charles Scribner's Sons, and solidified his power and influence with a series of *Century* articles he had developed and edited that were written by participants in the Civil War. The popularity of the articles had almost doubled the magazine's circulation and, hoping to repeat the success with a similar series on the California gold rush, he traveled to the Golden State in June 1889, to seek out and recruit forty-niners to write for him. At the same time, he hoped to realize a second goal for the trip, to convince John Muir to resume writing and contribute articles to the magazine—thereby scoring a major coup for *The Century* and for himself. After the writer had ignored his written appeals, the persistent editor requested Muir meet him at his San Francisco hotel.

Muir was late. Johnson waited in his room, dressed for a formal dinner party that was drawing nigh. He grew impatient, especially since the hotel had announced his guest's arrival some time before. Finally, he heard a voice echo down the hallway: "Johnson, Johnson! Where are you?" The seasoned explorer, who had hiked countless thousands of miles through the wilderness, who had navigated unfamiliar territory from one end of the continent to the other, had gotten lost in the hallways and passages of the hotel.

Muir could not have presented a picture more in contrast to the man in formal attire standing across the threshold of the posh room at the Palace Hotel. The caller's wind- and sunburned face was thin, hollow at the temples, framed by a disheveled gray-shot beard and floppy-brimmed black felt hat. The suit was dull and dark blue, the eyes bright and light blue.

Safe now in the confines of his host's room, the disoriented explorer told the editor that his absence from the literary world was owed to the consuming nature of managing the horticultural interests of his own and his aged in-laws' properties, along with raising two daughters. He expressed interest in returning to writing, and invited Johnson to visit him at the ranch, northeast across the bay, once his business in the city was finished. The editor agreed.

After a brief stop at the ranch, the pair packed up and set out for Yosemite so the Easterner could see what was happening to the California mountains and streams the writer so loved. What Muir showed him was not what Johnson had expected to see—much of the region had been logged off, grazed down, and burned over by unregulated and unrestricted logging and grazing. Ripe for a crusade, the two agreed to work together on a campaign to preserve and protect Yosemite by having it designated a national park, as Yellowstone had been. If Muir would write the articles to stir up public support, the editor would wield his influence and expertise as a lobbyist, which he had learned fighting for copyright laws, to generate political support.

The partnership rekindled both Muir's interest in the persuasive power of the written word and his enthusiasm for preserving nature. "The Treasures of the Yosemite" appeared in the August 1890 issue of *The Century* and "Features of the Proposed Yosemite National Park" in September. He had also provided his lobbyist partner with useful information for influencing politicians, including a map outlining his recommendations for the proposed park's boundaries and the features it should include.

General William Vandever, a congressman from Southern California, introduced legislation in the House of Representatives to establish Yosemite National Park, but at less than three hundred square miles, Muir and Johnson believed the proposed park too small to protect even a minimum of the area's splendor. A replacement bill was introduced, one which set the park's boundaries to include the entire drainage of the Tuolumne and Merced Rivers as well as some of the surrounding Sierra Nevada high country and nearby sequoia groves. The bill passed both the House and the Senate, and was signed into law by President Benjamin Harrison on October 1, 1890.

The convincing strength of the naturalist's writing, aided by the editor's equally powerful political maneuvering behind the scenes, accomplished all the crusading pair had set out to do. Muir's and Johnson's successful collaboration also kindled a long and productive relationship. The two worked together for years to come in the growing forest conservation movement as well as in the conception and publication of many magazine articles.

Muir's rediscovered enthusiasm for writing in the cause of wilderness preservation soon resulted in other periodical publications as well as a book, *The Mountains of California,* published in 1894. "I take pleasure in sending you with this a copy of my first book," Muir wrote to Jeanne Carr in November that year. "You will say that I should have written it long ago, but I begrudged the time of my young mountain-climbing days." Critically acclaimed upon release, the influential book sold well through many editions and remains in print to this day.

JOHN MUIR

In 1898, his conservation efforts were boosted further with a series of articles in *Harper's Weekly*. Another series in *The Atlantic Monthly* would later be collected, along with earlier writings on Yosemite, to become the book *Our National Parks*, published in 1901. Widespread attention and interest generated by his books and articles established Muir as an influential authority on wilderness preservation and forest protection, and his opinions and advice were sought by many, among them presidents of the United States.

Even with the benefit of long experience, the work of writing remained difficult. When invited by railroad millionaire Harriman to spend the summer of 1907 on the shores of Klamath Falls, Oregon, at his Pelican Bay Lodge, Muir declined, citing the time required and the difficulty of writing a book (most likely *My First Summer in the Sierra*). Harriman told him to come anyway, promising "I will show you how to write books." Like most who knew him, the industrialist was familiar with Muir's facility with the *spoken* word. So a shorthand secretary was assigned to shadow him and record his tales, which were then transcribed and typed onto more than a thousand pages. The pages were used, much later, as the basis of the book *The Story of My Boyhood and Youth*, first serialized in *The Atlantic Monthly*, then published in 1913.

Other books already written—or to be assembled afterward—would be published posthumously, but the final book Muir wrote was *Travels in Alaska*, an account of the first three of his many visits to the north country, drawn from his journals from the 1879, 1880, and 1890 expeditions. Much of 1914 was devoted to getting the book in order, and in December he packed up the pages and took them south with him to visit his daughter Helen Lillian and his new grandson on their ranch in California's Mojave Desert. He continued rewriting and editing even when he took ill there, was hospitalized in Los Angeles, and diagnosed with double pneumonia. Muir died Christmas eve 1914, alone at the hospital with the pages of the *Travels in Alaska* manuscript scattered about him on the bed.

Remembering Muir

J ohn Muir's influence on America did not die with him. His presence is yet felt throughout our society and culture. Honored in life, he has been honored more often, in more ways, in more places, since his death. Battles he initiated are still being waged, for, as he knew, the fight to preserve a wild place can be lost only once, but must be won repeatedly.

As an early and active inventor of the environmental movement, his ideas and philosophies still inspire millions around the world who have adopted many of his views as their own. The techniques he and his allies developed, employing both information and emotion to influence the public and the government, are still utilized. Organizations devoted to environmental protection today are numerous and their areas of emphasis diverse. Many, if not most, can trace their roots to the large and influential Sierra Club, which Muir helped found in 1892.

In his day, the American Academy of Arts and Letters

recognized his literary contributions, including numerous magazine articles and six books. Four other books were published posthumously. Most are still in print, and more popular today than when first published. Several other books have been published containing topical collections of Muir's writings gleaned from articles, essays, and excerpts from books and periodicals. His journals have been published, as well as collections of his correspondence. At least fifty biographies have been written, ranging from deep scholarly studies to short sketches for young readers, including one published in the Japanese language. He has also been the basis of characters in novels, the subject of stage plays and television documentaries, and the inspiration for more than a dozen songs.

While Muir was a lifelong student and scholar, his intermittent formal education and university study did not result in a diploma. Later, however, he had college degrees to spare—Harvard in 1896, the University of Wisconsin in 1897, Yale in 1911, and the University of California in 1913 awarded him honorary degrees.

His name continues to be tied to education. In California, a library and no fewer than twenty-one public schools, elementary through high school, carry his name. There is Muir College at the University of California at San Diego, and the John Muir Center for Regional Studies and John Muir Collections at the University of the Pacific in Stockton. In Wisconsin, his name is found on public schools in Madison, Portage, Milwaukee, and Wausau. On the campus at the University of Wisconsin in Madison is Muir Knoll, and the hand-carved mechanical study desk he invented for his own use and amusement is on display in the school's historical library. Beyond the states where he lived, schools are named for him Illinois, North Carolina, Ohio, Utah, and Washington state. Even in his native Scotland he is remembered by educators—Edinburgh University honored him with the John Muir Building, home to the Centre for the Study of Environmental Change and Sustainability.

Streets, roads, and highways across the country bear his name, as do government buildings, inns and lodges, hospitals, and city parks. His name is attached to natural wonders and places of scenic beauty, either to memorialize his association with that specific place, or to recognize his contributions to such places in general. At Alaska's Glacier Bay National Park is Muir Glacier, Muir Inlet, and Muir Point. Muir Woods National Monument is in Marin County, north of San Francisco. Also in California are Muir Gorge in Yosemite National Park; Muir Rock and Muir Pass in King's Canyon National Park; Sequoia National Park's Muir Grove, Muir Hut, Muir Lake, Muir Mountain, and Mount Muir; the John Muir Trail winds more than two hundred miles through the Sierra, including passage through the John Muir Wilderness. Other trails named for John Muir are in the Bronx, New York, Tennessee's Big South Fork National River and Recreation Area, and Wisconsin's Kettle Moraine State Forest. Camp Muir is in Mount Rainier National Park in the state of Washington, and there is a Muir Peak near Los Angeles, California.

While best remembered as an environmentalist, he was equally well-known in his time for his contributions to science, both in geology and botany, and recognized with membership in the Washington Academy of Science and fellowship in the American Association for the Advancement of Science.

Other scientific recognition is found in stone and on the wing. *Muirite* is an orange-colored mineral of the silicate family found in metamorphic rock in Fresno County, California. A bird, *Troglodytes troglodytes muiri*, or Muir's winter wren, lives in the coastal redwoods of California and Oregon. *Thecla muirii* is one of several previously unnamed species of butterflies first collected in the Sierra by the naturalist. Even a rodent, a subspecies of the pika found in Yosemite National Park, is designated *Ochotona princeps muirii* in his honor.

The scientific taxonomic and common English names of three plant species are named for Muir. *Ivesia muirii*, the granite mousetail, and Muir's tarweed, *Carlaquistia muirii* (previously *Raillardiopsis muirii*), are found in the Sierra; and *Erigeron muirii*, Muir's fleabane, is a delicate flower of the Aster family found near Cape Thompson in northwestern Alaska.

Many remember Muir as the "father of our national park system," recognizing his influence in the creation of many of our parks and obtaining national monument status (or other protection) for other wondrous places that would later become parks.

A series of articles Muir wrote for *The Atlantic Monthly* beginning in 1897 created widespread familiarity with national parks, and built public support and acceptance for their protection. "I have done the best I could to show forth the beauty, grandeur, and all-embracing usefulness of our wild mountain forest reservations and parks," he wrote of the essays, "with a view to inciting the people to come and enjoy them, and get them into their hearts, that so at length their preservation and right use might be made sure." The protection of vast tracts of public land that came to fruition during the administration of President Theodore Roosevelt owes at least a portion of its success to seeds planted by Muir.

In 1890, he directly petitioned President Benjamin Harrison to create Yosemite National Park to protect the area surrounding Yosemite Valley, which was then a state park and later absorbed into the national park. At the same time, he was instrumental in the designation of Sequoia National Park, which contains the General Sherman Tree, considered by some to be the largest living organism on earth. The park also includes Mount Whitney, the highest point in the continental United States. The 1890 initiative orchestrated with Muir's assistance also resulted in protection of the General Grant Grove of big trees, located in the Sierra between the two new national parks. The grove would later become the much larger King's Canyon National Park. In 1892, Muir and the newly organized Sierra Club successfully fought off an attack in Congress to essentially halve the size of Yosemite National Park, and repelled a similar attempt the following year.

His persuasive powers also helped create national parks protecting Mount Rainier in Washington State in 1899, Crater Lake in Oregon in 1902, Arizona's Petrified Forest in 1906, and Grand Canyon in 1908. His beloved Glacier Bay, in the angle of Alaska's panhandle, not declared a national park until 1925, had become widely known because of his credited discovery of the place in 1879 and the popular essays and articles that described his explorations there.

Other noteworthy recognition of Muir's contributions include United States postage stamps in 1964 and again in 1998. April 21 is "John Muir Day," officially designated in

1988 by a joint resolution of Congress and a proclamation by President Ronald Reagan. In January 2005, the United States Mint's California quarter, part of its fifty-state commemorative coin campaign, featured Muir hiking below Half Dome in Yosemite Valley.

Given the surprise he sometimes expressed at his fame and recognition while living, it is unlikely Muir could have known—or even suspected—that his memory, his influence, his ideas, his philosophies, would continue after his death. He did know, however, that *he* would continue. He wrote of death that "Myriads of rejoicing living creatures, daily, hourly, perhaps every moment sink into death's arms, dust to dust, spirit to spirit." Not gone, he said, but "waited on, watched over, noticed only by their Maker, each arriving at its own heaven-dealt destiny."

He knew, too, that the earth would abide. "This grand show is eternal," he wrote. "It is always sunrise somewhere; the dew is never all dried at once; a shower is forever falling; vapor is ever rising. Eternal sunrise, eternal sunset, eternal dawn and gloaming, on sea and continents and islands, each in its turn, as the round earth rolls."